I0797263

Disney

Enchanted Elixirs

Enchanted Elixirs

A MAGICAL COLLECTION OF TEAS, TONICS, SOUPS, SMOOTHIES, AND MORE

Thibaud Villanova

PHOTOGRAPHY
Nicolas Lobbestaël

STYLING
Sidonie Nalis

TRANSLATION
Lisa Molle Troyer

Once upon a time, there was a magical tome that held the secrets to savory soups, stews, and broths, bubbling cauldrons, and enticing spices: Welcome to Enchanted Elixirs!

I'm delighted and truly honored to be able to bring you a third culinary tribute to Disney and Pixar's most popular animated films.

Enchanted Recipes celebrated the many dishes cooked and enjoyed by beloved Disney characters, while Enchanted Baking focused on pastries and sweet treats. This third cookbook is dedicated to soups, stews, smoothies, and beverages that draw their inspiration from the most iconic scenes and characters from the world's greatest animation studio.

If you have any of my previous books, you know what I have in store for you: delicious, easy-to-make recipes; mouthwatering, immersive photography; and tips to guide you along the way—just like always.

If this is your first experience with one of my books, not to worry! Each is a stand-alone cookbook, and if Elixirs is the first step in your personal quest for a Disney meal, you haven't missed a thing. This book is designed for both new and experienced chefs. The aim of all my cookbooks is to help you bring your dreams to life with clearly explained recipes that let you linger a little longer in your favorite movie scenes. As Chef Gusteau says, "Anyone can cook!" I hope this book helps you believe and experience that for yourself, just like Remy does.

In these pages, you'll find recipes inspired by films ranging from *Snow White and the Seven Dwarves* and *Encanto* to *Treasure Planet*, *Cinderella*, *One Hundred and One Dalmatians*, *The Little Mermaid*, and many others. You can sit down to dinner with the family from Coco, make a soup that Pocahontas might have served, imagine how the evil Queen's potion would have tasted, and try the Clade family's soup or John Silver's bonzabeast stew. You'll also find plenty of tips and explanations of culinary terms so you can learn to cook while having fun.

It is such a privilege to bring you a third round of recipes from your favorite Disney and Pixar movies. I hope cooking them makes you smile and that the results are delicious.

Enjoy the book, and bon appétit!

Thibaud Villanova
Gastronogeek

CONTENTS

THE PRINCESSES

BASIC EQUIPMENT
P. 14

ELIXIR EQUIPMENT
P. 16

WHAT IS AN ELIXIR?
P. 18

CINDERELLA
MIDNIGHT LATTE
Pumpkin spice latte with chocolate-hazelnut whipped cream
P.22

SLEEPING BEAUTY
A ROYAL VINTAGE
Spiced grape juice with blackberry syrup
P. 24

ALADDIN
ARABIAN NIGHTS JALLAB
Homemade date syrup with rose water
P. 26

MOANA
MOTUNUI COOLER
Coconut, guava, and kiwi smoothie
P. 28

BRAVE
A POTION TO CHANGE YOUR FATE
Strawberry, blueberry, cran-apple, and mint smoothie
P. 30

TANGLED
HAZELNUT PARSNIP WHIP
Vanilla-hazelnut milkshake with whipped cream and caramelized parsnip chips
P. 32

THE LITTLE MERMAID
A DEVIOUS POTION
Blueberry, pomegranate, and grape juice blend with coconut whipped cream
P. 34

SNOW WHITE AND THE SEVEN DWARFS
THE QUEEN'S TRANSFORMATION POTION
Cream of mint and watercress soup with chili pepper
P. 36

THE PRINCESS AND THE FROG
CREAMY GUMBO-STYLE SOUP
Cream of pepper soup with smoked sausage
P. 38

BEAUTY AND THE BEAST
PORRIDGE AND TABLE MANNERS
Overnight oats with raspberries and pistachios
P. 42

POCAHONTAS
HARVEST SOUP
Corn chowder
P. 44

RAYA AND THE LAST DRAGON
KUMANDRA SOUP
Tom yum soup
P. 46

Global Cuisine

HERCULES
HERCULADE CITRUS TWIST
Homemade cola with citrus
P. 50

TOY STORY
ALIEN JELLIES
Mint and green tea jellies
P. 52

THE RESCUERS DOWN UNDER
A TOAST TO BERNARD!
Lemon-lime soda, yuzu, and ginger
P. 54

INSIDE OUT
FREEEZE!
Strawberry-watermelon smoothie
P. 56

HERCULES
MORTALITY POTION
Pear, pomegranate, grape, and blueberry smoothie
P. 58

THE EMPEROR'S NEW GROOVE
MAGIC POTION
Cherry, strawberry, mint, and basil syrup
P. 60

PINOCCHIO
RUSTIC RIBOLLITA
Italian-style bread soup with vegetables
P. 62

LILO AND STITCH
SURF'S UP SMOOTHIE
Pineapple, mango, and lime smoothie
P. 64

LILO AND STITCH
SURF'S UP SHAVE ICE
Grated frozen fruit
P. 65

BIG HERO 6
LUCKY CAT CAFÉ RAMEN
Miso ramen with marinated egg and barbecue bacon
P. 68

LUCA
ZUPPA MARCOVALDO!
Fish and seafood stew
P. 72

COCO
MOLE RIVERA
Mexican mole sauce with hazelnuts
P. 74

ENCANTO
AJIACO
Flavorful broth with corn and cilantro
P. 78

ROBIN HOOD
NOTTINGHAM POTTAGE
Poached chicken in a vegetable broth with homemade garlic croutons
P. 80

RATATOUILLE
THE SOUP
Remy's Velouté du Barry
P. 82

THE RESCUERS DOWN UNDER
CHANDELIER PEA SOUP
Cream of pea soup with chervil and lemon
P. 84

TURNING RED
BREAKFAST PORRIDGE
Rice congee with ginger, jujube, and kumquats
P. 86

PETER PAN
SOOTHING NIGHTCAP
Linden blossom, chamomile, and orange blossom tea with honey
P. 88

ONE HUNDRED AND ONE DALMATIANS
BLACK AND WHITE BOBA
Homemade bubble tea with Earl Grey, orange blossom, and almond milk
P. 90

THE SWORD IN THE STONE
SAINT-TROPEZ SPECIAL
Peach, apricot, and grapefruit juice with tonic water
P. 92

CONTENTS

Fantasy Worlds

ZOOTOPIA
CARROT TONIC
Carrot, ginger, and apple shake
P. 96

ALICE IN WONDERLAND
WONDERLAND POTION
Pineapple-cherry juice
P. 98

TREASURE PLANET
BONZABEAST STEW
Lobster, shrimp, and clams in saffron broth
P. 100

STRANGE WORLD
THE CLADES' DANCING SOUP
Roasted vegetable soup
P. 104

THE FOX AND THE HOUND
WIDOW TWEED'S COZY NOG
Brioche-infused eggnog
P. 106

FROZEN
SUMMER IN A CUP
Lemon-lime soda with orange and grape juice
P. 108

TIPS

SEASONAL FRUITS AND NUTS
P. 112

SEASONAL VEGETABLES
P. 114

STOCKS

Vegetable Stock
P. 116

Fish Stock
P. 116

Chicken Stock
P. 117

SAUCES AND CONDIMENTS

Marinated Eggs
P. 118

Barbecue Sauce
P. 118

Lobster Bisque
P. 119

A LITTLE SOMETHING SWEET

Hazelnut and Chocolate Chip Cookies
P. 120

Whipped Cream
P. 120

Vanilla Ice Cream
P. 121

Hazelnut Praline Paste
P. 122

Applesauce
P. 123

SIMPLE TWISTS ON YOUR DRINKS

Colorful Ice Cubes
P. 124

Fruity Ice Cubes
P. 124

CONVERSIONS
P. 125

GLOSSARY
P. 126

INGREDIENT INDEX
P. 128

AFTERWORD
P. 136

BASIC EQUIPMENT

Hand mixer

Blender

Saucepan

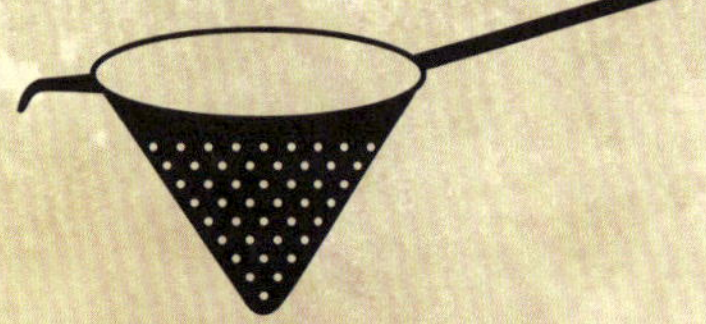
Strainer

Dutch oven

Paring knife

Mixing bowl

Star tip

Stewpot

Whisk

Ladle

Silicone spatula

Immersion blender

Pastry brush

Piping bag

Frying pan

Stand mixer

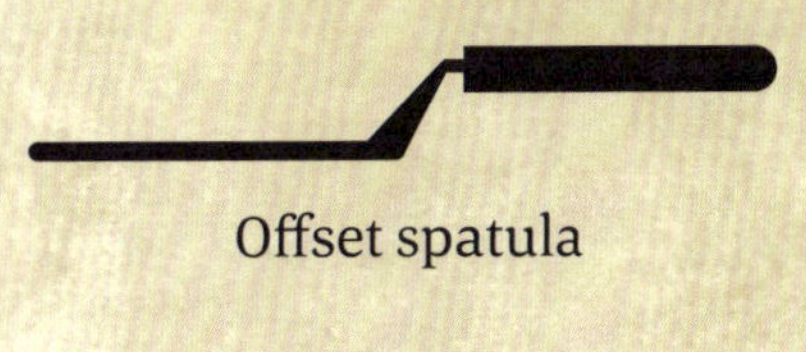

Offset spatula

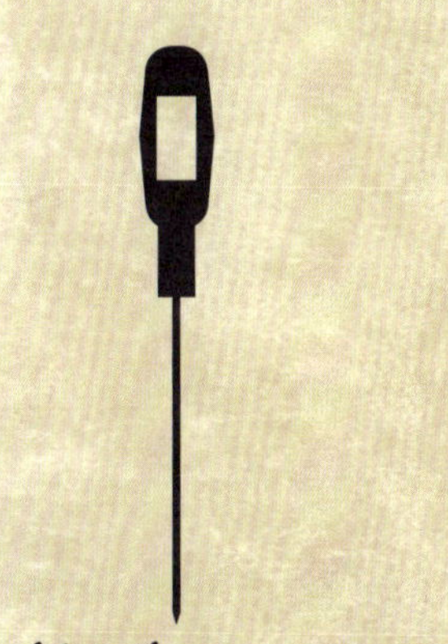

Cooking thermometer

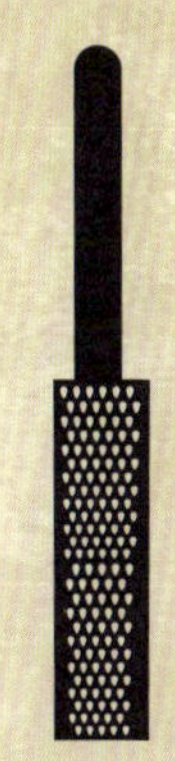

Zester

Soup tureen

ELIXIR EQUIPMENT

Bowl

Chawan
(tea bowl)

Teapot

Boston shaker

Citrus press

Coffee mug

Three-piece shaker

Metal goblet

Potion vial

Laboratory flask

Tea cup

Tumbler

Square tumbler

Milkshake glass

Smoothie cup

Iced tea glass

Julep cup

Tulip glass

WHAT IS AN ELIXIR?

What are elixirs? How is a soup different from a stock? Or a milkshake different from a smoothie?

Here are a few culinary terms to help you speak the secret language of liquids.

- **Stock** is a flavorful liquid made by simmering ingredients like bones, meat, vegetables, herbs, and spices in water for a long time. It is used as a base for soups, sauces, and many other dishes.
- There are a wide variety of stocks for different purposes, from different cuisines and different cultures. French and Western cuisines often use chicken, vegetable, and meat stock. The foundation for Japanese cuisine is dashi, a broth made from kombu seaweed and dried bonito flakes.
- A **soup** is various ingredients—such as vegetables, meat, or fish—cooked in water or stock. Soup may contain large pieces of ingredients.
- In a **blended soup**, the cooked ingredients have been puréed together for a smooth, even consistency.

- When a soup is described as "**cream of**" an ingredient, it generally means that a roux or cream has been added to create a thicker, smoother texture than a standard soup.
- A **smoothie** is a thick, creamy beverage made by blending fresh fruit with milk, plant-based milk, fruit juice, or yogurt. A **milkshake** has a similar texture to a smoothie, but it contains more dairy.
- A **mocktail** is a non-alcoholic cocktail. Mocktails employ the same techniques and ingredients used in traditional mixology to create a flavorful, refreshing drink without the alcohol.
- A **juice** is a liquid extracted from a fruit or vegetable and enjoyed fresh, with or without additional flavoring. Recipes may also refer to the aromatic liquid extracted from a vegetable, meat, or fish as juices.

THE PRINCESSES

MIDNIGHT LATTE

PUMPKIN SPICE LATTE WITH CHOCOLATE-HAZELNUT WHIPPED CREAM

Cinderella has always been associated with pumpkins, and this cozy pumpkin spice drink is a fitting tribute to an enchanted carriage and a glittering evening at the royal ball.

DIFFICULTY

Prep time: 10 minutes
Cook time: 30 minutes

INGREDIENTS

Yield: 4 servings

½ butternut squash
2 teaspoons ground ginger
2 cups whole milk
1 stick cinnamon
1 star anise
3 tablespoons maple syrup
4 shots of espresso

CHOCOLATE-HAZELNUT WHIPPED CREAM

¾ cup plus one tablespoon heavy whipping cream, cold
2 tablespoons mascarpone
3 tablespoons chocolate-hazelnut spread (I recommend Nocciolata®)

EQUIPMENT

Steamer pot
Immersion blender
Hand mixer or whisk

1. Peel the half squash and cut it into cubes. Cook the cubes in the steamer pot for 20 minutes. When they are soft all the way through, move the butternut cubes to a mixing bowl. Use a potato masher to smash into a smooth, even butternut purée. Season with the ground ginger and set aside.
2. Pour the milk into a saucepan. Add the cinnamon, star anise, and maple syrup. Bring the mixture to a simmer and stir well. Leave the spices to steep for 10 minutes and then use a skimmer or strain the mixture to remove them. Add the butternut purée to the spice-infused milk and then use the immersion blender to blend until smooth. Keep warm over very low heat while you make the chocolate-hazelnut whipped cream.
3. TO MAKE THE CHOCOLATE-HAZELNUT WHIPPED CREAM: Pour the cold whipping cream into a mixing bowl. Use a whisk or hand mixer to whisk the cream vigorously until stiff and then add the mascarpone and chocolate-hazelnut spread as you continue to whisk. Whisk briefly until you have a rich, decadent whipped cream!

FINISHING TOUCHES

Divide the butternut latte between 4 mugs. Add 1 shot of espresso to each mug and top with chocolate-hazelnut whipped cream. Serve right away.

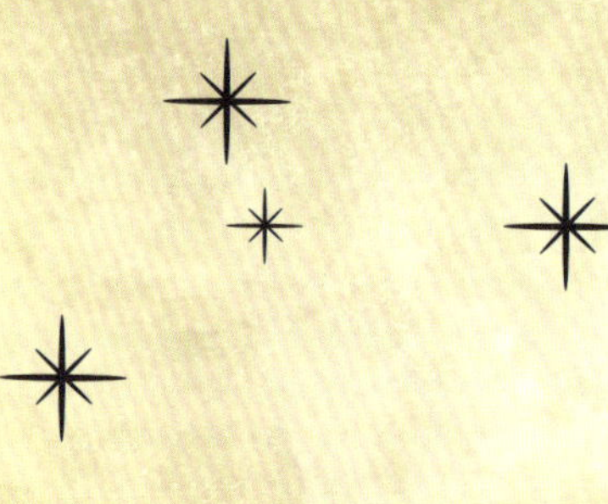

A ROYAL VINTAGE

SPICED GRAPE JUICE WITH BLACKBERRY SYRUP

DIFFICULTY

Prep time: 15 minutes
Cook time: 15 minutes

INGREDIENTS

Yield: 1 liter

3¾ cups grape juice
1 orange
1-inch piece fresh ginger
2 sticks cinnamon
1 star anise
2 cloves
2 tablespoons blackberry syrup

This is just the type of drink that King Stefan and King Hubert might have filled their glasses with to toast their children's engagement.

1. First, pour the grape juice into a saucepan and warm it over low heat. Zest the orange and slice it into rounds. Add the orange zest and rounds to the saucepan.
2. Rinse the ginger and smash it by placing it under a cutting board and striking it with the palm of your hand.
3. Add the ginger to the saucepan along with the cinnamon sticks, star anise, cloves, and blackberry syrup. Simmer the mixture over medium heat for 15 minutes, taking care not to let it boil.
4. Serve piping hot!

ARABIAN NIGHTS JALLAB

HOMEMADE DATE SYRUP WITH ROSE WATER

DIFFICULTY

Prep time: 15 minutes
Resting time: 3 hours
Cook time: 30 minutes

INGREDIENTS

Yield: 4 glasses and 1 bottle of date syrup

18 ounces medjool dates
4 teaspoons rose water
Ice cubes, for serving

EQUIPMENT

Fine mesh strainer

Dates, a desert delicacy very popular in Agrabah, can also be made into a sweet syrup. When flavored with spices and diluted with water, this syrup becomes a refreshing beverage and a tonic for mind and body. Here's how to make it yourself.

1. Place the dates in a mixing bowl, add water to cover, and leave to soak for 3 hours. Drain off the excess water and transfer the dates to a Dutch oven. Add ¾ cup water and bring to a boil.
2. Cook the dates at a slow boil for 10 to 12 minutes and then use a spoon or fork to press as much juice as possible out of them. Strain.
3. To concentrate the juice, pour it into a saucepan and cook over medium heat for several minutes until the juice takes on a syrup-like consistency. You can store this date syrup in a small bottle or airtight jar.
4. To make one glass of jallab, dilute 1 tablespoon date syrup in ½ cup still or sparkling mineral water, add 1 teaspoon rose water, stir, and add ice cubes to chill. Enjoy!

MOTUNUI COOLER

COCONUT, GUAVA, AND KIWI SMOOTHIE

DIFFICULTY

Prep time: 10 minutes

INGREDIENTS

Yield: 4 servings

2 guavas
¾ cup coconut water, chilled
2 kiwis
Juice of 1 lime
1 cup coconut milk
4 tablespoons crushed ice

EQUIPMENT

Blender
Fine mesh strainer

Motunui is a tropical island where coconuts grow in abundance. The locals appreciate their sweet milk, refreshing water, and useful husks and leaves. This refreshing drink celebrates the village of Motunui and its coconuts, which give the islanders all they need.

1. First, peel and coarsely chop the guavas. Add them to the blender along with the coconut water and blend on high for 15 seconds until smooth. Filter with a fine mesh strainer to remove the seeds and pulp.
2. Rinse out the blender and then pour the guava juice back in.
3. Peel and quarter the kiwis and add them to the guava juice in the blender, along with the lime juice, coconut milk, and crushed ice. Blend on high for 30 seconds for a refreshing smoothie.
4. Serve right away and enjoy your tropical treat!

A POTION TO CHANGE YOUR FATE

STRAWBERRY, BLUEBERRY, CRAN-APPLE, AND MINT SMOOTHIE

DIFFICULTY

Prep time: 10 minutes

INGREDIENTS

Yield: 4 servings

4 large fresh strawberries
2 tablespoons fresh blueberries
2 tablespoons Applesauce, storebought or homemade (see recipe on page 123)
Dash of peppermint syrup
2 cups cranberry juice
A few ice cubes
A few mint leaves

EQUIPMENT

Blender

It's not easy to change your fate—you have to be willing to do whatever it takes, even if that means making some sacrifices. You also need to be a master of the magical arts, able to brew potions with great precision, or there's no telling what might happen. You might turn your own mother into a bear!

1. First, rinse the strawberries under a little running water. Hull and quarter them. Rinse the blueberries and carefully pat dry. Place the fruit in a blender.
2. Add the applesauce, peppermint syrup, cranberry juice, and ice cubes.
3. Blend on high for 30 seconds until smooth. Garnish each glass with a few fresh mint leaves and serve right away.
4. Enjoy!

HAZELNUT PARSNIP WHIP

VANILLA-HAZELNUT MILKSHAKE WITH WHIPPED CREAM AND CARAMELIZED PARSNIP CHIPS

DIFFICULTY

Prep time: 10 minutes
Cook time: 30 minutes

INGREDIENTS

Yield: 4 servings

1 parsnip
2 tablespoons brown sugar
2½ cups Vanilla Ice Cream, storebought or homemade (see recipe on page 121)
2½ cups whole milk
2 tablespoons Hazelnut Praline Paste, storebought or homemade (see recipe on page 122)
¾ cup Whipped Cream, storebought or homemade (see recipe on page 120)
2 Hazelnut and Chocolate Chip Cookies, storebought or homemade (see recipe on page 120), crushed
Grapeseed oil, for brushing
Salt, for sprinkling

EQUIPMENT

Pastry brush
Potato masher
Blender

Over the years she lived in her tower, Rapunzel had plenty of time to bake dozens of cookies and eat bowls and bowls of the parsnip and hazelnut soup that Mother Gothel would bring her. This recipe brings together all those flavors in one deliciously unique drink.

1. Preheat the oven to 350°F and bring a small pot of water to a boil.
2. Rinse and dry the parsnip. Cut it in half. Place half of the parsnip into the water and cook at a gentle boil for 15 minutes.
3. Thinly slice the other half and arrange the slices on a baking sheet lined with parchment paper. Use a pastry brush to lightly coat both sides of the parsnip slices with grapeseed oil. Sprinkle very lightly with salt and brown sugar. Bake the parsnip slices for 15 minutes to caramelize. Remove from the oven and set aside.
4. When the boiled parsnip is soft all the way through, drain it and mash with a potato masher. Set aside the purée.
5. Add the ice cream, milk, praline paste, and parsnip purée to a blender and blend on high for 20 seconds until smooth, cold, and creamy.

FINISHING TOUCHES

Pour immediately into 4 large milkshake glasses. Top each glass with a generous serving of whipped cream and sprinkle with crushed cookies and caramelized parsnip chips. Serve right away.

A DEVIOUS POTION

BLUEBERRY, POMEGRANATE, AND GRAPE JUICE BLEND WITH COCONUT WHIPPED CREAM

DIFFICULTY

Prep time: 10 minutes

INGREDIENTS

Yield: 1 large glass

WHIPPED CREAM

7 tablespoons coconut cream, for whipping

1 tablespoon honey

POTION

7 tablespoons red grape juice

7 tablespoons pomegranate juice

2 tablespoons blueberry jam or purée

1 tablespoon crushed ice

EQUIPMENT

Hand mixer or whisk

Piping bag with a round tip

Blender

Beware what lurks in the darkest shadows of the ocean deep—especially Ursula, no matter how tempting her offers may seem. And that goes double for her potions. Luckily, this drink worthy of a sea witch has no hidden strings attached.

1. TO MAKE THE WHIPPED CREAM: Pour the coconut cream into a mixing bowl and whisk vigorously using a hand mixer or whisk. As the cream starts to become firm, drizzle in the honey while continuing to whisk.
2. Transfer the whipped cream to the piping bag fitted with a round tip and set aside in a container in the refrigerator.
3. TO MAKE THE POTION: Pour the grape juice, pomegranate juice, and blueberry purée or jam into a blender with the crushed ice. Blend on high for 20 seconds and then pour the mixture into a tall sundae glass.
4. Garnish with whipped cream and a straw and serve right away.

THE QUEEN'S TRANSFORMATION POTION

CREAM OF MINT AND WATERCRESS SOUP WITH CHILI PEPPER

DIFFICULTY

Prep time: 10 minutes
Cook time: 30 minutes

INGREDIENTS

Yield: 4 servings

2 Yukon Gold potatoes
1 large onion
2 bunches watercress
10 mint leaves plus 2 more for garnishing
2 tablespoons olive oil
1 teaspoon table salt
1½ teaspoons ground pepper
6 cups Vegetable Stock, storebought or homemade (see recipe on page 116)
1 tablespoon ricotta
Pinch of ground Calabrian chili pepper
4 teaspoons coarse salt

EQUIPMENT

Immersion blender or regular blender

The people of the kingdom would never imagine that their beautiful and powerful Queen has a wicked workshop hidden deep in the castle, where she stores her spell books and prepares her potions and poisons. This delicious recipe may resemble her infamous transformation potion, but it is perfectly harmless.

1. Peel the potatoes and cut into ½-inch cubes. Peel and finely chop the onion. Rinse the watercress, leaving in place the rubber band or twist tie holding the bunches together. Rinse the mint leaves and pat dry with a paper towel. Now that your mise en place is finished, you are ready to start cooking.

2. Warm the olive oil in a cast iron Dutch oven or stewpot over medium heat. Add the chopped onion and sauté for 2 minutes before adding the potatoes. Season with salt and pepper, sauté for another 2 minutes, and add the stock. Bring to a simmer and cook for 20 minutes.

3. Meanwhile, blanch the watercress: Prepare a large bowl of ice water. Boil 8 cups of water with the coarse salt. When the water is boiling, drop in the bunches of watercress. Remove after 20 seconds and transfer immediately to the ice water. Drain the bunches, untie them, and finely chop the watercress. Add it to the stock with the potatoes and onion.

4. Remove the Dutch oven from the heat, add the mint leaves, and blend the soup for 30 seconds, either with an immersion blender or by transferring the entire mixture to a blender, until it is smooth and green. Add the ricotta and chili pepper and blend again to combine. Adjust seasoning. Serve this creamy soup either very hot or chilled, garnished with fresh mint leaves.

CREAMY GUMBO-STYLE SOUP

CREAM OF PEPPER SOUP WITH SMOKED SAUSAGE

DIFFICULTY

Prep time: 15 minutes
Cook time: 45 minutes

EQUIPMENT

Immersion blender or regular blender

Gumbo is a Creole stew from Louisiana that Tiana's father used to make for her when she was a child. It's hot, flavorful, and spicy, and warms both the body and the heart. This recipe turns the traditional dish into a creamy soup with the taste of New Orleans.

1. Preheat the oven broiler to 425°F.
2. First, arrange the peppers on a baking sheet lined with parchment paper. Bake for 20 to 25 minutes until the skin is thoroughly blackened, which will make the peppers easier to peel and give them a smoky flavor.
3. While the peppers are in the oven, prepare the rest of the ingredients: Peel and finely chop the onion. Dice the celery. Peel, de-germ, and chop the garlic cloves. Finally, cut the smoked sausages into small cubes. Now that your mise en place is finished, you're ready to start cooking.
4. Add the smoked sausage to a cast iron Dutch oven or a skillet that is still cold—starting with a cold pan allows the sausages to release their fat and caramelize. Turn on the heat to medium and cook the sausages for 10 minutes. Remove 2 tablespoons of sausage cubes and set aside on a paper towel to use as a garnish.
5. Add the onion and celery to the Dutch oven and cook for another 5 minutes, stirring well to incorporate the caramelized bits from the sausages and brown the vegetables. Next, add the garlic and cook for 1 more minute, taking care not to burn it.
6. Your aromatics are hard at work by now, making the dish smell like gumbo already.

INGREDIENTS

Yield: 4 servings

2 red bell peppers
1 large onion
1 stalk celery
2 cloves garlic
2 smoked sausages
1½ tablespoons butter
2½ tablespoons flour
1 teaspoon ground cumin
1 teaspoon ground sweet paprika
1 teaspoon cayenne or milder chili pepper
⅔ cup Fish Stock, storebought or homemade (see recipe on page 116)
9 ounces whole peeled tomatoes, canned
2 cups Lobster Bisque, storebought or homemade (see recipe on page 119)
A few leaves flat-leaf parsley
Salt

7. Add the butter. When it has melted, sprinkle in the flour, cumin, paprika, chili pepper, and a pinch of salt. As you stir them over the heat, the flour and butter will combine to form a "roux," a classic thickener used in French cuisine. Stir well to combine, then deglaze with the fish stock. Continue to stir until smooth.

8. Next, add the peeled tomatoes with their juice and the bisque. Check the seasoning and add more salt if necessary. Turn the heat down to low and hold the soup at a gentle boil.

9. Taking care not to burn yourself, remove the charred peppers from the hot oven and arrange them on your work surface. Cover with a lid or a piece of plastic wrap and set aside for several minutes, allowing condensation to form and fall on the peppers, which will make them easier to peel. Deseed and peel the peppers. Chop them into large pieces and add to the Dutch oven.

10. Finally, blend the soup with an immersion blender until thick, smooth, and creamy.

FINISHING TOUCHES

Divide between 4 soup plates. Arrange a few leaves of parsley and some cubes of smoked sausage on each bowl. Enjoy!

PORRIDGE AND TABLE MANNERS

OVERNIGHT OATS WITH RASPBERRIES AND PISTACHIOS

DIFFICULTY

Prep time: 15 minutes
Resting time: 9 hours minimum, and up to 72 hours

INGREDIENTS

Yield: 4 servings

1¾ cups rolled oats
½ cup plus 1 tablespoon Skyr
¾ cup plus 1 tablespoon coconut milk
1 teaspoon rose water
¼ cup unsalted shelled pistachios
½ cup raspberries
5 teaspoons honey (or maple or agave syrup)
2 teaspoons dried rose petals

Sitting down to a meal with someone is the perfect way to get to know them better—Lumière's dinner entertainment certainly reveals a lot about his personality! At the Beast's castle, even the simplest meal, like breakfast for two, could show that there's something there that wasn't there before.

1. This decadent oatmeal is very easy to make and requires no cooking. You can prepare it the night before, and it will be ready to eat in the morning.
2. Stir together the rolled oats, Skyr, and coconut milk in a bowl. Add 1 teaspoon of honey. Mix thoroughly and stir in the rose water.
3. Crush the pistachios and cut about two-thirds of the raspberries in half. Carefully fold the pistachios and raspberry halves into the oat mixture with a wooden spoon. Cover and refrigerate for at least 9 hours.

FINISHING TOUCHES

Divide the overnight oats between 4 soup plates. Drizzle each serving with 1 teaspoon of honey and garnish with the whole raspberries and a few rose petals. Enjoy!

HARVEST SOUP

CORN CHOWDER

DIFFICULTY

Prep time: 20 minutes
Cook time: 45 minutes

INGREDIENTS

Yield: 4 servings

- 2 shallots
- 1 carrot
- 1 potato
- 2 ears sweet corn
- 3 tablespoons butter
- 2 tablespoons flour
- 4 cups Vegetable or Chicken Stock, storebought or homemade (see recipes on pages 116–117)
- ¾ cup heavy whipping cream
- 2 teaspoons sweet paprika
- 2 teaspoons black pepper
- 1¼ teaspoons salt
- Olive or grapeseed oil, for brushing
- A few leaves flat-leaf parsley

EQUIPMENT

Immersion blender or regular blender

Corn is a staple food for the Powhatan people, and its grains can be used to make many things. One of the tastiest is corn chowder, a nourishing and flavorful dish popular throughout North America.

1. Preheat the oven broiler to 425°F or preheat your charcoal grill.
2. Peel and finely chop the shallots. Peel the carrot and potato and cut into ½-inch cubes. Shuck the corn.
3. Bring a large pot of water to a boil and cook the ears of corn for 10 to 12 minutes, then drain. Dry the corn and brush with olive or grapeseed oil. Roast the corn in the oven broiler or on the grill for 25 minutes, turning it regularly to brown on all sides.
4. Meanwhile, prepare the rest of the chowder: Place the butter in a Dutch oven and melt over medium heat. Add the shallots and sweat for 10 minutes over medium-low heat, stirring frequently. Add the carrot and potato and sprinkle with a pinch of salt. Stir well, dust with the flour, and stir again. Pour in the stock gradually while continuing to stir. Stir in the cream.
5. When the corn is roasted, remove the kernels from the cobs. Add ¾ of the kernels to the Dutch oven with the vegetables and stock. Set the rest aside for garnishing.
6. Use an immersion blender to blend the contents of the Dutch oven into a smooth, flavorful soup. Season to taste with pepper and the remaining salt and add the paprika. Stir well. The chowder is ready to serve.
7. Pour the corn chowder into 4 bowls and garnish each with a few parsley leaves and some grilled corn kernels. Serve piping hot!

KUMANDRA SOUP

TOM YUM SOUP

DIFFICULTY

Prep time: 15 minutes
Cook time: 20 minutes

INGREDIENTS

Yield: 4 servings

2 stalks lemongrass
⅔ cup bamboo shoots
2 small Thai chili peppers
1 bundle shimeji mushrooms
1 teaspoon palm sugar
1 teaspoon shrimp paste
3 lime leaves
2 tablespoons nuoc mam (fish sauce)
Juice and zest of 2 limes
1¼ teaspoons salt
½ bunch fresh cilantro, for garnishing

Nothing brings people together like a good meal or a good bowl of soup. That's why Chief Benja teaches his daughter to make a special soup using one ingredient from every kingdom in Kumandra. The rich broth takes its flavor from products grown by each of the different clans, and it symbolizes unity and reconciliation. Now you can make it for yourself!

1. First, bring 4 cups of water to a boil in a large saucepan.
2. Cut the base off the lemongrass stalks and use the heel of your hand or the back of a spoon to smash them along their entire length. This will loosen the fibers of the lemongrass and release as much flavor as possible into the soup. Discard the 2 thick outer layers of the lemongrass and cut the core into fine matchsticks. Slice the bamboo shoots into rounds.
3. Cut the chili peppers into diagonal slices. For a less spicy soup, remove the seeds first. Set the chili peppers slices aside in a bowl and wash your hands thoroughly. Take care not to touch your eyes or face with fingers that have touched chili peppers. Slice the mushrooms off at the base of the bundle and set aside.
4. Warm a Dutch oven over medium heat and add the mushrooms and chili pepper. Cook for 2 minutes, while stirring, to brown the mushrooms and release the flavor from the chili peppers. Reducing the heat to low if necessary so that nothing burns. Sprinkle with the palm sugar and stir well. Add the pungent shrimp paste and then the boiling water. Stir well.
5. Lastly, add the lime leaves, lemongrass, fish sauce, bamboo shoots, and lime zest and juice. Stir well and add the salt. Adjust seasoning to taste. Cook at a gentle boil for 15 minutes.
6. Divide the Kumandra Soup between 4 bowls. Sprinkle each bowl with fresh cilantro and serve right away.

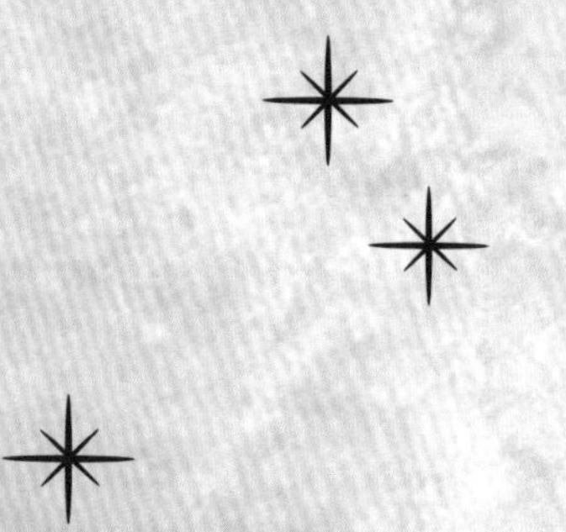

Global Cuisine

HERCULADE CITRUS TWIST

HOMEMADE COLA WITH CITRUS

DIFFICULTY

Prep time: 15 minutes
Cook time: 12 minutes
Resting time: 1 hour

INGREDIENTS

Yield: 4 servings

1⅓ cups brown sugar
⅔ cup water lukewarm water
1 tablespoon lemon juice
Juice and zest of 1 pink grapefruit
Juice and zest of 1 mandarin (Chios if possible)
1 teaspoon vanilla extract
1 star anise
1-inch piece fresh ginger
2 cups sparkling water or lemon-lime soda, very cold

EQUIPMENT

Fine mesh strainer

There are many versions of the refreshing beverage that mere mortals know as Herculade. This one features the sweet-tart flavors of citrus varieties from all over Greece.

1. Add the brown sugar, water, and lemon juice to a saucepan. (The lemon juice will keep the sugar from crystallizing.) Melt the sugar over low heat and then cook at a gentle boil for 7 to 10 minutes until the mixture is smooth, thick, and a rich golden brown.

2. Add the citrus zest and juice to the saucepan with the caramel, along with the vanilla extract and star anise. Stir and continue to cook over low heat. Mince the ginger and add it to the mixture. Stir well and cover. Remove from the heat and steep for 30 minutes at room temperature, then refrigerate for another 30 minutes.

3. When the caramel mixture is thoroughly infused with flavor, strain it into a pitcher and add the cold sparkling water or lemon-lime soda. Serve with ice cubes or crushed ice.

Feel the power of the gods of Olympus coursing through your veins!

ALIEN JELLIES

MINT AND GREEN TEA JELLIES

DIFFICULTY

Prep time: 10 minutes
Cook time: 10 minutes
Resting time: 4 hours

INGREDIENTS

Yield: 8 jellies

1 bag gunpowder green tea
2½ tablespoons mint syrup
1 drop green food coloring
2 teaspoons gelatin powder
Cooking spray or grapeseed oil, for greasing

EQUIPMENT

8 individual small molds

Haven't you always wanted to make jellies that look like the Toy Story *aliens?*

1. Bring 2 cups plus 2 tablespoons of water to a boil in a saucepan. Remove the saucepan from the heat and add the bag of green tea. Let steep for 2 minutes and then remove the tea bag. You should have 2 cups of green tea.
2. Add the mint syrup and green food coloring to the saucepan and bring to a boil. Whisk in the gelatin powder and continue to whisk for 1 minute. Remove the saucepan from the heat and set aside.
3. Use the cooking spray or a pastry brush and some grapeseed oil to lightly grease the molds. This will make it easier to remove the jellies.
4. Arrange the molds on a baking sheet. Fill them with the mixture. Let rest for 30 minutes at room temperature and then refrigerate for 3 hours and 30 minutes, or until the jelly has set.
5. Serve your alien jellies when firm.

A TOAST TO BERNARD!

LEMON-LIME SODA, YUZU, AND GINGER

DIFFICULTY

Prep time: 5 minutes

INGREDIENTS

Yield: 2 glasses

3 tablespoons ginger juice
1½ tablespoons maple syrup
3 tablespoons yuzu juice
4 large ice cubes
⅔ cup lemon-lime soda, very cold
2 strips lime zest

EQUIPMENT

Boston shaker
2 stemmed glasses

When Bernard joined the Rescue Aid Society, who would have guessed he would end up going on so many adventures with Miss Bianca? Who could have imagined they would become such a dynamic duo? Let's raise our glasses and toast these brave mice!

1. Pour the ginger juice, maple syrup, yuzu juice, and ice cubes into the Boston shaker equipped with a strainer. Close the shaker and shake vigorously for 10 to 15 seconds to chill.
2. Strain the mixture into 2 glasses. Dilute with cold lemon-lime soda and garnish each glass with 1 strip of lime zest.
3. Serve very cold.

YOUR

FREEEZE!

STRAWBERRY-WATERMELON SMOOTHIE

DIFFICULTY

Prep time: 10 minutes

INGREDIENTS

Yield: 4 servings

4 fresh strawberries
14 ounces watermelon
¾ cup plus 2 tablespoons strawberry juice
⅓ cup plus 2 tablespoons chilled coconut water
1 tablespoon sugar
10 ounces crushed ice

EQUIPMENT

Blender

This deliciously fruity smoothie will cool you right down, just like the frigid ponds and skating rinks of Minnesota where you used to play hockey with your friends. Such fond memories!

1. First, rinse the strawberries under a little running water. Hull and quarter them. Remove the watermelon rind and cut the flesh into large pieces.
2. Place the fruit in a blender along with the strawberry juice, coconut water, and sugar.
3. Blend on high for 30 seconds until thick and smooth.
4. Add the crushed ice and blend for another 10 seconds to chill the smoothie.
5. Serve immediately and enjoy!

MORTALITY POTION

PEAR, POMEGRANATE, GRAPE, AND BLUEBERRY SMOOTHIE

DIFFICULTY

Prep time: 10 minutes

INGREDIENTS

Yield: 4 servings

2 Bosc pears
Seeds from 1 pomegranate
2 cups grape juice
2 tablespoons blueberry syrup
A few ice cubes

EQUIPMENT

Blender
Fine mesh strainer

The god of the underworld is not about to let the birth of Zeus's son disrupt his plans. A baby will not stand between him and the throne on Mount Olympus! But he may regret sending his minions to handle the problem...

This version of the potion Hades makes for baby Hercules is completely safe and perfectly delicious.

1. First, peel and core the pears. Chop the fruit and add it to the blender. Add the pomegranate seeds, grape juice, blueberry syrup, and ice cubes to the blender as well.
2. Blend on high for 45 seconds until smooth and chilled.
3. Strain and serve right away.

MAGIC POTION

CHERRY, STRAWBERRY, MINT, AND BASIL SYRUP

DIFFICULTY

Prep time: 15 minutes
Cook time: 15 minutes

INGREDIENTS

Yield: 2½ cups syrup

7 ounces cherries
5 ounces strawberries
1½ cups sugar
1¼ cups mineral water
6 basil (or huacatay) leaves
2 mint leaves

The evil sorceress Yzma is humiliated after the Emperor fires her, and she has more than one trick—and potion—up her sleeve to get revenge. Why not try to reproduce one of her many transformation spells for yourself?

1. Rinse, de-stem, and pit the cherries. Cut each in half. Thoroughly rinse the strawberries, then hull and chop them.
2. Add the fruit to a deep, thick-bottomed saucepan or a Dutch oven. Add the sugar, water, and herbs. Stir well and heat to a simmer.
3. Continue to cook at a gentle boil for 10 minutes, then use a fork to smash the fruit before cooking for another 5 minutes.
    - For a crystal-clear syrup, strain the mixture and transfer to an airtight bottle. This syrup can be kept for several weeks.
    - If you prefer the texture of a fruit purée, blend the contents of the saucepan together before pouring into an airtight bottle.
4. Your potion is ready!

GOOD TO KNOW

The syrup or fruit purée can be diluted in water or lemon-lime soda, added to a cocktail or mocktail, or drizzled over cake.

RUSTIC RIBOLLITA

ITALIAN-STYLE BREAD SOUP WITH VEGETABLES

DIFFICULTY

Prep time: 15 minutes
Cook time: 1 hour

INGREDIENTS

Yield: 4 servings

9 ounces canned navy beans (or dry, rehydrated for several hours)
4 leaves lacinato kale
1 carrot
2 large potatoes
2 stalks celery
2 onions
2 cloves garlic
2 tablespoons olive oil
¼ cup white wine
7 ounces whole peeled San Marzano tomatoes, canned
5 cups Vegetable Stock, storebought or homemade (see recipe on page 116)
1 sprig fresh rosemary
2 sprigs fresh thyme
1 bay leaf
4 slices rustic bread
2 tablespoons pine nuts
A few fresh basil leaves, for garnishing
Salt and pepper, for seasoning

This Tuscan vegetable soup will warm your heart, just like the soup simmering in a cast-iron pot on the hearth in Geppetto's workshop.

1. Drain and rinse the beans. Set aside. Rinse, dry, and thinly slice the kale. Peel and dice the carrot, potatoes, celery, and onions. Peel, de-germ, and crush the garlic.
2. Pour the olive oil into a Dutch oven and warm over medium heat. When the oil is very hot, add the onion, carrot, and celery and cook for 10 minutes, taking care not to brown them too much. Add the garlic and cook for another 2 minutes. Add the potatoes and kale. Season lightly with salt and pepper and stir well. Deglaze with the white wine and reduce for 5 minutes before adding the tomatoes and vegetable stock.
3. Lastly, add the beans and herbs. Check the seasoning, cover the pot, and then cook for 45 minutes at a gentle simmer.

FINISHING TOUCHES

Place 1 slice of bread into each bowl or soup plate and ladle generous servings of vegetable soup over top. Arrange a few pine nuts and fresh basil leaves on each bowl. Enjoy!

SURF'S UP SMOOTHIE

PINEAPPLE, MANGO, AND LIME SMOOTHIE

DIFFICULTY

Prep time: 5 minutes

INGREDIENTS

Yield: 4 servings

1 small pineapple
1 fresh mango
Juice and zest of 1 lime
⅔ cup water
A few ice cubes

EQUIPMENT

Blender

Enjoy this delicious smoothie with your ohana after a day catching waves off the beautiful beaches of Kauai.

1. Cut off the top of the pineapple and remove the peel. Cut it into large pieces. Peel the mango and cut the flesh off the pit.
2. Add the fruit and other ingredients to a blender and blend on high for 30 seconds. Serve very cold.

GOOD TO KNOW

For a sweet twist on this recipe, try adding coconut ice cream or lemon sorbet.

SURF'S UP SHAVE ICE

GRATED FROZEN FRUIT

DIFFICULTY

Prep time: 10 minutes
Resting time: 12 hours

INGREDIENTS

Yield: 2 servings

1 small pineapple
1 fresh mango
Zest and juice of 1 lime

EQUIPMENT

Microplane® zester or cheese grater

Lilo and Stitch have definitely enjoyed more than a few bowls of shave ice. Here's a unique twist on the popular Hawaiian dessert.

1. Peel the pineapple and mango and freeze for 12 hours.
2. Work quickly when it's time to prepare your dessert: Use a Microplane® zester or cheese grater to grate the frozen pineapple and mango into 2 bowls.
3. Sprinkle with lime zest and drizzle with lime juice. Serve right away.

LUCKY CAT CAFÉ RAMEN

MISO RAMEN WITH MARINATED EGG AND BARBECUE BACON

DIFFICULTY

Prep time: 20 minutes
Cook time: 30 minutes

Located in San Fransokyo, an imaginary city that blends American and Japanese culture, Aunt Cass's Lucky Cat Café serves delicious homestyle fusion dishes inspired by the two countries. Ramen dishes are definitely on the menu!

1. Preheat the oven broiler to 350°F.
2. First, coat the bacon slices with barbecue sauce. Arrange them on a baking sheet lined with parchment paper. Bake for 12 minutes.
3. Peel the ½ sweet potato and chop it into large cubes. Coat the cubes with grapeseed oil, arrange on another baking sheet lined with parchment paper, and bake for 12 minutes. Remove the baking sheet from the oven, brush the sweet potatoes with the maple syrup, and then return them to the oven for 3 more minutes to finish baking. Set aside.
4. Meanwhile, finely chop the spring onion and then make the broth: In a saucepan, heat the vegetable or chicken stock to a simmer. In a bowl, stir the miso into the soy sauce to dissolve it. Add the contents of the bowl to the stock. Hold the broth at a simmer while you cook the noodles.

INGREDIENTS

Yield: 4 servings

8 slices smoked bacon or 4 slices pork belly
2 tablespoons high-quality Barbecue Sauce, storebought or homemade (see recipe on page 118)
½ sweet potato
1 tablespoon maple syrup
1 spring onion
6 cups Vegetable or Chicken Stock, storebought or homemade (see recipes on pages 116–117)
2 tablespoons red or white miso paste
3 tablespoons soy sauce
4 servings instant or fresh ramen noodles
2 Marinated Eggs (ajitsuke tamago, see recipe on page 118)
4 sheets dried nori
4 drops sesame oil
Grapeseed oil, for brushing

5. Bring a large pot or 4 small saucepans full of water to a boil. Drop in the ramen noodles and cook for 2 minutes (or according to the package directions). Drain the noodles and divide between 4 bowls. Assemble the soup immediately.

6. Pour the simmering broth over the noodles. Divide the barbecue bacon, roasted sweet potato cubes, and spring onion between the bowls. Cut each egg in half and place ½ egg in each bowl. Finally, garnish with nori and finish with a single drop of sesame oil in each bowl. Serve right away.

ZUPPA MARCOVALDO!

FISH AND SEAFOOD STEW

DIFFICULTY

Prep time: 20 minutes
Cook time: 30 minutes

INGREDIENTS

Yield: 4 servings

½ fennel bulb
2 shallots
2 cloves garlic
3 tablespoons olive oil, divided
4 Yukon Gold potatoes
2 teaspoons coarse salt
6 cups Fish Stock, storebought or homemade (see recipe on page 116)
⅓ cup white wine
9 ounces San Marzano tomatoes, canned
1 teaspoon sugar
1 sprig fresh thyme
1 sprig fresh rosemary
4 fillets white fish, such as rockfish
7 ounces cod fillet
8 large shrimp or prawns, peeled and deveined
1 teaspoon salt, plus more to taste
2 teaspoons pepper
2½ cups garlic bread croutons
Olive oil, for drizzling

Massimo Marcovaldo may not be a man of many words, but his cooking speaks volumes. He is an excellent fisherman who knows just how to prepare his catch. This fish stew is inspired by the Italian cuisine of Luca.

1. Preheat the oven to 350°F.
2. Clean the ½ fennel bulb and cut it into thick slices. Peel and finely chop the shallots. Peel, de-germ, and thinly slice the garlic.
3. Arrange the fennel slices on a baking sheet lined with parchment paper. Drizzle lightly with olive oil and sprinkle with a pinch of salt. Bake for 20 minutes.
4. Meanwhile, prepare the potatoes. Rinse them and then drop into a pot of cold water. Add the coarse salt and bring to a boil. Boil for 15 minutes. Drain and peel the potatoes, using a fork to prick and a paring knife to peel them so as not to burn yourself. Leaving the skins on the potatoes while they cook keeps them from getting waterlogged. If you prefer, you can peel them before cooking. Quarter the potatoes and set aside.
5. Warm the fish stock in a pot over medium heat until it begins to simmer.
6. Pour a drizzle of olive oil into a Dutch oven and warm over medium heat. Add the chopped shallots. Sauté the shallots in the oil over medium heat for 2 minutes and then add the garlic and quartered potatoes. Stir well and deglaze with the white wine. Cook to reduce before adding the tomatoes with their juice. Season with salt and pepper to taste and then add the sugar. Add the thyme, rosemary, and fish stock. Cook at a gentle simmer for 10 minutes and then drop the fish and shrimp or prawns into the Dutch oven. Poach for 3 minutes and then divide the stew between 4 soup plates.

FINISHING TOUCHES

Add a slice of the roasted fennel and some garlic bread croutons to each bowl. Serve piping hot!

MOLE RIVERA

MEXICAN MOLE SAUCE WITH HAZELNUTS

DIFFICULTY

Prep time: 30 minutes
Cook time: 1 hour 30 minutes

EQUIPMENT

Spice grinder
Skimmer or spider strainer
Blender
Chinois strainer

INGREDIENTS

It has been a long time since they enjoyed such a lively feast, but after Miguel travels to the Land of the Dead and heals a generational heartbreak, his family is once again able to gather around a table laden with delicious dishes. This mole sauce is inspired by the Mexican culture celebrated in Coco.

1. First, prepare the peppers: De-stem them and then remove and set aside the seeds.
2. Rinse, dry, hull, and quarter the tomatoes (and tomatillos, if using). Peel and quarter the onion. Peel and de-germ the garlic. Next, begin the first round of cooking.
3. Heat the stock to a simmer in a large pot.
4. Add the pepper seeds and sesame seeds to a dry frying pan. Toast for 2 minutes over medium heat, taking care not to burn them. Add the other spices and continue to toast for another 2 minutes. Transfer the toasted spices to the spice grinder and grind into a fragrant powder. Set aside.
5. Pour the grapeseed oil into a Dutch oven and heat it to 285°F to 300°F. Drop in the dried peppers for 3 to 4 minutes to soften. Scoop them out with a skimmer or spider strainer and transfer to a large mixing bowl.
6. Now drop the almonds, hazelnuts, and pepitas into the hot oil. Fry the nuts for 2 minutes, then remove and add them to the bowl with the peppers.
7. Drop the apricots and raisins into the oil for 2 minutes, then remove and add to the bowl with the other ingredients.
8. Cook the garlic in the hot oil for 30 seconds to 1 minute to just brown, then remove it and add to the other ingredients.
9. Cook the onion in the hot oil for 2 minutes, then remove it and add to the other ingredients.
10. Cook the tomato quarters (and tomatillo, if using) for 2 to 4 minutes and then transfer to the bowl with the other ingredients.
11. Finally, break the bread into pieces, fry for 1 minute, and then add to the other ingredients.

Yield: 8 cups of sauce

4 ancho peppers
2 pasilla peppers
1 or 2 mulato peppers
2 tomatoes plus 2 tomatillos (or 2 more tomatoes)
1 large onion
2 cloves garlic
7 cups Vegetable or Chicken Stock, storebought or homemade (see recipes on pages 116–117)
4 tablespoons sesame seeds
2 cloves
1 stick cinnamon
1 star anise
1 teaspoon cumin seeds
1 teaspoon black pepper
1 tablespoon dried oregano
3¼ cups grapeseed oil or frying oil
⅓ cup unsalted almonds
⅓ cup hazelnuts
4 tablespoons pepitas
2 tablespoons dried apricots
2 tablespoons raisins
1 slice day-old bread
3 teaspoons salt
2½ teaspoons brown sugar
1½ ounces dark chocolate

12. You can now filter the richly flavored oil and store it in a jar or bottle to be used later in a sauce, as a condiment, or for cooking. Set the Dutch oven aside to be used in the second round of cooking—no need to wash it.
13. Transfer the fried ingredients, the ground toasted spices, and the hot stock to a blender, working in two batches so as not to overfill the blender. Blend on high for 1 minute.
14. Strain the resulting mixture into the Dutch oven.
15. You should have a thick, creamy sauce. Add the salt and brown sugar and adjust to taste. Finally, crush the chocolate into small pieces and add it to the sauce.
16. Stir well and simmer for 1 hour over low heat, stirring regularly.
17. Your mole sauce is ready. Serve it with chicken or tortillas, or as a condiment with soup or salad.

GOOD TO KNOW

While this recipe is not difficult, you do need to be patient and organized. Some mole recipes have dozens of ingredients, and others are perpetual moles that are fed every day like a sourdough starter. I hope you make this simple version your own as you experiment over time.

If you aren't used to cooking with chili peppers, make sure to handle them with gloves or wash your hands regularly. You can burn yourself by rubbing your eyes or touching your face after handling peppers or pepper seeds.

AJIACO

FLAVORFUL BROTH WITH CORN AND CILANTRO

DIFFICULTY

Prep time: 30 minutes
Cook time: 45 minutes

INGREDIENTS

Yield: 4 servings

1 spring onion
4 russet potatoes
2 Jerusalem artichokes
½ bunch fresh cilantro
2 ears corn
1 teaspoon ground cumin
1 teaspoon ground sweet paprika
1½ tablespoons dried oregano
2 chicken tenderloins
5 cups Chicken Stock, storebought or homemade (see recipe on page 117)
1 cup heavy whipping cream
2 avocados
1 tablespoon capers
Olive oil, for cooking
Salt and pepper

If want a meal that's fantastical and magical, just sit down to dinner with the family Madrigal! Here is a twist on a traditional ajiaco Colombiano that Julieta and her family might have served.

1. First, peel and finely chop the onion. Peel the potatoes and Jerusalem artichokes and cut into ½-inch cubes. Remove the cilantro leaves from the stems and set aside both stems and leaves. Shuck the corn and cut each ear into 2 round sections. Set aside.
2. Pour a drizzle of olive oil into a mixing bowl and add the cumin, paprika, dried oregano, a pinch of salt, and a pinch of pepper. Mix well and then add the chicken tenderloins. Coat them with the spice mixture. Set aside.
3. Warm a Dutch oven over medium heat. When it is hot, add the chicken and brown for 2 minutes on each side. Add the spring onion, potatoes, Jerusalem artichokes, corn, and cilantro stems. Lightly salt the vegetables and stir well.
4. Increase the heat to high for a few moments and pour in the chicken stock. Stir well, bring to a simmer, and cook for 10 to 12 minutes.
5. Remove the chicken from the Dutch oven and continue to cook the soup for another 4 to 5 minutes. Reduce the heat to low.
6. Shred the chicken using 2 forks and return it to the Dutch oven. Stir in the cream and check the seasoning. Lightly salt if necessary. Set aside over low heat.
7. Peel, pit, and cube the avocados. Now, serve the soup.

FINISHING TOUCHES

Divide the ajiaco between 4 soup plates, making sure to put the same amount of meat, vegetables, and broth in each. Sprinkle the avocado cubes and capers over each bowl and add the fresh cilantro leaves. Enjoy!

NOTTINGHAM POTTAGE

POACHED CHICKEN IN A VEGETABLE BROTH
WITH HOMEMADE GARLIC CROUTONS

DIFFICULTY

Prep time: 20 minutes
Cook time: 30 minutes

INGREDIENTS

Yield: 4 servings

½ farm-raised chicken, cleaned and broken down by the butcher (or 1 small whole chicken)
2 large onions
4 small young carrots
2 cloves garlic
1 bunch Swiss chard
4 baby turnips
1 large russet potato
1 clove
3½ tablespoons butter
1 tablespoon sunflower oil
1 tablespoon flour
8½ cups Vegetable Stock, storebought or homemade (see recipe on page 116)
Salt and pepper

CROUTONS

½ baguette, slightly stale
10 leaves flat-leaf parsley
1 clove garlic
2 tablespoons butter

Life is not easy for the English under the rule of greedy Prince John. It's especially hard for the people of Nottingham, who must somehow feed themselves despite constant extortion by the corrupt Sheriff of Nottingham. They make do with the help of Robin and his band, finding humble ingredients to cook.

1. First, lightly salt the chicken on all sides. Set aside.
2. Peel and halve the onions. Roast 1 half onion by placing it cut side down in a frying pan over medium heat, and cut the other half into quarters or thick slices. Peel the carrots. Peel, de-germ, and crush the garlic. Clean the Swiss chard and cut into pieces slightly larger than 1 inch. Clean the turnips and chop their leaves. Peel the potato and chop into cubes. Now you are ready to begin cooking.
3. Warm a Dutch oven over medium heat. Add the clove and toast for 2 minutes, then add the butter and sunflower oil. Melt the butter and add the chicken. Brown it for 2 minutes on each side before adding all the vegetables. Lightly salt and pepper the ingredients. Sprinkle with the flour and add vegetable stock to cover. Stir well and bring to a gentle boil. Cover and simmer for 35 minutes.
4. TO MAKE THE CROUTONS: Cut the stale bread into small cubes. Finely chop the parsley. Peel, de-germ, and chop the garlic.
5. Melt the butter over low heat in a frying pan. Add the garlic and parsley followed by the bread cubes. Fry for 2 to 3 minutes, making sure to thoroughly coat the cubes with the butter and other ingredients. When the croutons are nicely browned, transfer them to a paper towel.

FINISHING TOUCHES

To serve, divide the vegetables, chicken, broth, and croutons evenly between four soup plates or bowls. Enjoy!

THE SOUP

REMY'S VELOUTÉ DU BARRY

DIFFICULTY

Prep time: 15 minutes
Cook time: 25 minutes

INGREDIENTS

Yield: 4 servings

1 cauliflower
4 teaspoons coarse salt
10 fresh chives
10 stems flat-leaf parsley
2 cloves garlic
5½ tablespoons Beurre d'Isigny butter
¾ teaspoon sugar
1 cup Chicken Stock (see recipe on page 117)
1 teaspoon salt, plus more to taste

EQUIPMENT

Potato masher
Blender

Remy learned everything he knows about cooking from Chef Gusteau's classic dishes. He channels his passion—and a few lessons from the famous chef—to help young Linguini transform a basic soup into a refined masterpiece. Now you can learn to make this classic French soup, too.

1. First, prepare the cauliflower. Rinse and cut into florets. Transfer to a Dutch oven and add water to cover. Add the coarse salt. Cover and bring to a gentle boil. Cook for 10 minutes, until the cauliflower is tender all the way through.
2. Meanwhile, continue your mise en place by preparing the herbs: Finely chop the chives and parsley. Peel, de-germ, and finely chop the garlic. Set aside.
3. When the cauliflower is cooked, use a skimmer to scoop it out. Set aside 2 cups of the cooking water—which has absorbed the flavor of the cauliflower—and discard the rest.
4. Transfer the cauliflower florets to a mixing bowl and use a potato masher to mash into a thick cauliflower purée. Set aside.
5. Melt the butter over medium heat in a stewpot. Add the cauliflower purée, salt, and sugar, and stir to combine. Caramelize the purée by cooking it over medium-low heat for 10 minutes, stirring often. When the purée turns golden brown, add the chicken stock and the saved cauliflower cooking water. Pour the mixture into a blender and blend for 5 minutes.
6. Transfer the creamy mixture back to the Dutch oven and warm over low heat. Add the herbs and season to taste. Serve piping hot!

GOOD TO KNOW

This cream of cauliflower soup is delicious with a poached egg and a drop of walnut oil.

CHANDELIER PEA SOUP

CREAM OF PEA SOUP WITH CHERVIL AND LEMON

DIFFICULTY

Prep time: 5 minutes
Cook time: 20 minutes

INGREDIENTS

Yield: 4 servings

14 ounces fresh garden peas, shelled
1 large russet potato
2 spring onions
10 stems fresh chervil
3 tablespoons butter
3¼ cups Vegetable or Chicken Stock, storebought or homemade (see recipes on pages 116–117)
1 teaspoon sugar
Juice and zest of 1 lemon
⅔ cup heavy whipping cream
1 teaspoon salt, plus more to taste

EQUIPMENT

Immersion blender or regular blender

What would the guests at a high society dinner think if they knew that a second Society was also enjoying a fancy meal right above their heads—including soup made with the very same peas?

1. Rinse the fresh peas. Peel the potato and cut into ½-inch cubes. Peel and finely chop the spring onions. Finely chop the chervil.
2. Prepare a large mixing bowl of ice water. Bring a large pot of salted water to a boil. Drop the peas into the boiling water for 4 minutes and then immediately transfer them to the ice water. After 30 seconds, drain them and set aside.
3. Place the butter in a Dutch oven or large saucepan and warm it over medium heat. Sauté the onions and potatoes for 2 minutes. Add a pinch of salt and stir well. Add just enough stock to cover and continue to cook for another 15 minutes.
4. Add the peas, sugar, lemon juice and zest, chervil, and the remaining stock. Stir well and then use an immersion blender to create a smooth soup.
5. Stir in the cream and blend again for several seconds. If the soup seems too thick, add more water or stock to thin. Check the seasoning and add salt if necessary.
6. Serve immediately and enjoy!

WALES
LISMORE

BREAKFAST PORRIDGE

RICE CONGEE WITH GINGER, JUJUBE, AND KUMQUATS

DIFFICULTY

Prep time: 20 minutes
Cook time: 30 minutes

INGREDIENTS

Yield: 4 servings

1 stalk lemongrass
6 cremini mushrooms
1½-inch piece fresh ginger
5 cups Vegetable or Chicken Stock, storebought or homemade (see recipes on pages 116–117)
1 dried jujube
Scant ⅔ cup short-grain rice
2 kumquats

Mei's mother, Ming, wants her daughter to be perfect. Just imagine if she found out that Mei had turned into a red panda! Mei is so grateful for the burned pot of congee that distracted her mother at just the right moment. Here's how to make your own congee inspired by the movie—without burning it!

1. Congee is a porridge of rice cooked in a flavorful broth until it is very soft. First, make the broth: Cut the base off the lemongrass stalk and use the heel of your hand or the flat side of a knife to smash it along its entire length to break the fibers. Discard the 2 outer layers of the lemongrass and cut the rest into fine matchsticks. Set aside.
2. Wipe off the mushrooms with a damp paper towel. Cut them into thin slices. Rinse and dry the ginger, leaving the skin on, and thinly slice the whole thing. Now you are ready to begin cooking.
3. Bring the stock to a boil and add the lemongrass, ginger, mushrooms, and jujube. Add the short-grain rice. Sitr well and cook over high heat for 3 minutes. Reduce the heat to low and simmer for 35 to 40 minutes at a gentle boil.
4. When the rice is very soft, remove the jujube and press the rice into the cooking liquid. Your mushroom and lemongrass congee is ready!

FINISHING TOUCHES

Divide the piping hot congee between 4 bowls and zest the kumquats over it just before serving.

SOOTHING NIGHTCAP

LINDEN BLOSSOM, CHAMOMILE, AND ORANGE BLOSSOM TEA WITH HONEY

DIFFICULTY

Prep time: 5 minutes

INGREDIENTS

Yield: 1 teapot

2½ cups spring water

2 heaping teaspoons dried chamomile

2 heaping teaspoons dried linden blossom

1 drop bitter orange essential oil

2 drops passionflower extract

1 teaspoon wildflower honey

EQUIPMENT

Tea ball strainer

It's not always easy to go to bed when you are bubbling over with energy and imagination, like the Darling children. Luckily, Nana always brings a tray of tonics to help them drift off to sleep. This soothing herbal concoction will soon have you on your way to Neverland.

1. Pour the water into a saucepan and bring to a simmer.
2. Place the dried chamomile and linden blossom in a tea ball strainer.
3. Pour the hot water into a teapot, add the bitter orange essential oil, passionflower extract, and honey, and stir well. Finally, add the tea ball and steep for 5 minutes to make a calming, soothing infusion.
4. Serve hot.

BLACK AND WHITE BOBA

HOMEMADE BUBBLE TEA WITH EARL GREY, ORANGE BLOSSOM, AND ALMOND MILK

DIFFICULTY

Prep time: 10 minutes
Cook time: 20 to 30 minutes

INGREDIENTS

Yield: 4 servings

1⅔ cups spring water
1 bag Earl Grey tea
4 drops orange blossom extract
6 tablespoons large black tapioca pearls (not instant)
3 tablespoons maple or agave syrup
2½ cups almond milk
A few ice cubes

This unique tea is a nod to the beautiful spots on a Dalmatian's coat.

1. Bring the water to a simmer and pour it into a teapot. Add the bag of Earl Grey, steep for 2 minutes, and then remove the bag. Add the orange blossom extract and set the tea aside at room temperature.
2. Now, prepare the tapioca pearls: Bring a large pot of water to a boil and cook the tapioca pearls for 20 to 30 minutes. Drain the tapioca pearls, rinse with cold water, and transfer to a bowl.
3. Pour the syrup over the tapioca pearls and set aside.
4. Finally, make your bubble tea: Scoop 1 tablespoon of black tapioca pearls into a bubble tea cup. Add ice cubes, then pour in ¼ of the almond milk.
5. Fill with the orange blossom-flavored tea.
6. Repeat with the 3 other cups and enjoy right away.

SAINT-TROPEZ SPECIAL

PEACH, APRICOT, AND GRAPEFRUIT JUICE WITH TONIC WATER

DIFFICULTY

Prep time: 5 minutes

INGREDIENTS

Yield: 1 glass

⅓ cup peach purée
⅓ cup apricot juice
1½ tablespoons grapefruit juice
3 tablespoons crushed ice
¼ cup cold tonic water
A few fresh verbena leaves
1 slice pink grapefruit

EQUIPMENT

Shaker

The wizard Merlin is wise, powerful, and a little loony. One of his many powers is the ability to travel through time and space. This is exactly the sort of drink he might have enjoyed on his last trip to Saint-Tropez.

1. Add the peach purée, apricot juice, and grapefruit juice to a shaker. Add the crushed ice and close the shaker. Shake vigorously for no more than 10 to 15 seconds to blend and chill the mixture.
2. Pour into a glass and dilute with the tonic. Use a cocktail spoon to stir the drink in the glass.
3. Garnish the cocktail with the verbena leaves and a grapefruit slice.
4. Serve very cold.

FANTASY WORLDS

CARROT TONIC

CARROT, GINGER, AND APPLE SHAKE

DIFFICULTY

Prep time: 5 minutes

INGREDIENTS

Yield: 4 servings

1 green apple
2½ cups carrot juice
2¾ tablespoons ginger juice
1 teaspoon turmeric
1 tablespoon plus 1 teaspoon simple syrup
A few ice cubes
8 tablespoons crushed ice

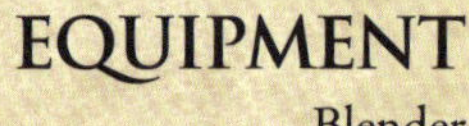

EQUIPMENT

Blender

Every bunny from Bunnyburrow knows absolutely everything about carrots, from how to grow them to how to eat them—in cakes, gratins, soups, or salads; juiced, steamed, roasted, braised, glazed, and so on. This energizing carrot drink might just give you the boost you need to leave your hometown and strike out on an adventure!

1. First, deseed the apple. Add it to the blender along with the ice cubes.
2. Add the carrot and ginger juice, turmeric, simple syrup, and ice cubes and blend on high for 30 seconds. Strain and divide between 4 glasses.
3. Add 2 tablespoons of crushed ice to each glass before serving.

POLICE
FRESH

WONDERLAND POTION

PINEAPPLE-CHERRY JUICE

DIFFICULTY

Prep time: 5 minutes

INGREDIENTS

Yield: 4 servings

1 cup pineapple juice
Juice and zest of ½ lime
1 tablespoon cherry purée
2¾ tablespoons cherry syrup
1 or 2 drops pink food coloring (optional)
2 cups lemon-lime soda

EQUIPMENT

Boston shaker or blender

If you asked Alice about the flavor of the shrinking potion that she drank, she would tell you it tasted first of cherry and then of pineapple. Curious, don't you think? Let's try to make a drink like that for ourselves.

1. First, pour the pineapple juice, lime juice and zest, cherry purée, and cherry syrup into a Boston shaker or blender. Add pink food coloring for a more vibrant color, if desired.
2. Blend or shake vigorously for 30 seconds.
3. Divide the mixture between 4 glasses, dilute with the lemon-lime soda, and serve. Try garnishing the glasses with a maraschino cherry and pineapple wedge.

BONZABEAST STEW

LOBSTER, SHRIMP, AND CLAMS IN SAFFRON BROTH

DIFFICULTY

Prep time: 20 minutes
Cook time: 30 minutes

EQUIPMENT

Fine mesh strainer

While he claims to be a simple cook, John Silver looks more like a grizzled old sailor, with his cybernetic eye and mechanical leg. The way he talks and acts suggests he might be hiding something—but whatever it is, it's not his talent as a chef. His bonzabeast stew looks delicious! Here's a recipe you can make here on our planet.

1. This recipe requires a little patience, but there is nothing difficult about it. First, prepare the mise en place for the vegetables: Peel and finely chop the shallots. Peel, de-germ, and chop the garlic. Peel the carrots and slice into rounds. Finely chop the parsley.

2. Next, prepare the shellfish and clams: Drop the clams into a basin of cold water along with a handful of salt for 10 minutes to purge.

3. Meanwhile, peel and devein the shrimp, setting aside the shells, heads, and carcasses. Repeat for the lobster. Cut the lobster meat into 4 pieces and set aside in the refrigerator. Drain the clams and rinse well under cold water.

4. Add 1 tablespoon grapeseed oil and 2 tablespoons of the butter to a Dutch oven. Melt over medium heat. Add the saved shellfish carcasses and crush into small pieces with a rolling pin to release as much flavor as possible.

INGREDIENTS

Yield: 4 servings

4 shallots
4 cloves garlic
2 carrots
½ bunch flat-leaf parsley
7 ounces clams
7 ounces raw shrimp or prawns
1 prepared lobster
1 tablespoon grapeseed oil
5½ tablespoons butter
1 bouquet garni (4 parsley stems, 1 fennel frond, 1 bay leaf, and 1 sprig of thyme tied in a green leek leaf)
2 saffron threads
6 cups Fish Stock, storebought or homemade (see recipe on page 116)
¾ cup heavy whipping cream
1 teaspoon ground sweet paprika (optional)
3 tablespoons olive oil
Scant ½ cup white wine
1 tablespoon Armagnac
2 teaspoons salt, as needed
2 teaspoons pepper, as needed

5. Add the carrots, parsley, and bouquet garni. Add a pinch of salt and one turn of the pepper shaker as well as the saffron. Increase the heat to high and brown the ingredients for 2 minutes, stirring frequently, before pouring in the fish stock. Stir well and cook for 15 minutes. Strain and add the flavorful liquid back into the Dutch oven. Pour in the cream and stir well. Season to taste and keep warm over very low heat.

6. Finally, add the olive oil and the remaining butter to a separate Dutch oven or stewpot and warm over medium heat. When the butter is melted, add the shallots and brown for 2 minutes before adding the garlic. Add the clams and deglaze with half the white wine. Cover the pot and cook over medium heat for 4 minutes, covered. When the clams have opened, remove them from the Dutch oven and add the shrimp and lobster meat. Season with salt and pepper. Add the paprika, if using. Sauté for another 2 minutes and then deglaze with the remaining white wine. Stir well and use a wooden spatula to scrape the browned bits from the bottom of the Dutch oven. Reduce the white wine, then add the Armagnac and flambé. When the alcohol has evaporated and the flames have died down, add the hot, creamy fish broth. Get ready to plate.

FINISHING TOUCHES

Divide the clams and pieces of lobster meat between 4 soup plates. Pour in the flavorful broth and add some shrimp to each plate. Serve right away.

THE CLADES' DANCING SOUP

ROASTED VEGETABLE SOUP

DIFFICULTY

Prep time: 10 minutes
Cook time: 30 minutes

INGREDIENTS

Yield: 4 servings

1 mild green chili pepper
1 teaspoon salt, plus more to taste
1 sprig fresh thyme
1 sprig fresh rosemary
¾ cup Vegetable Stock, storebought or homemade (see recipe on page 116)
1 teaspoon tomato paste
2 teaspoons Espelette pepper or paprika
¾ teaspoon sugar
2 teaspoons pepper, as needed
A few leaves flat-leaf parsley
¼ cup olive oil, plus more for garnishing

EQUIPMENT

Blender

When the Clades cook, they reach for farm-fresh produce seasoned with plenty of joy, love, and laughter. The family loves to put on a record and dance as they work together to make delicious dishes, like this summer vegetable soup.

1. Preheat the oven to 375°F.
2. Rinse the zucchinis and cut off the blossom ends. Slice 1 zucchini into thick rounds. Peel and de-germ the garlic. Peel the onions. Rinse the tomatoes, bell peppers, and chili. Deseed 1 of the bell peppers and cut into strips. Arrange the zucchini, garlic, onions, tomatoes, bell peppers, and chili (both cut and whole) in a casserole dish. Drizzle generously with ¼ of olive oil. Use 1 teaspoon of salt to season the vegetables evenly and then tuck in the thyme and rosemary.
3. Bake for 25 minutes, removing the zucchini rounds from the dish halfway through. After 25 minutes, move the dish to the top rack of the oven and broil for 1 minute 30 seconds.
4. Remove the casserole dish from the oven. Remove and set aside the bell pepper strips. Discard the thyme and rosemary stems.
5. Cut the stalks off the whole bell pepper and the chili. Transfer the entire contents of the casserole dish to a blender and blend on high for 1 minute 30 seconds.
6. Your roasted vegetable purée is ready. Add vegetable stock to thin to your preferred texture. Add the tomato paste, Espelette pepper or paprika, and sugar. Season with pepper. Blend on high for 10 seconds until smooth.

FINISHING TOUCHES

Arrange the roasted bell pepper strips and zucchini rounds in 4 bowls or soup plates. Fill with roasted vegetable soup. Sprinkle with a few parsley leaves and add a light drizzle of olive oil. Enjoy!

GOOD TO KNOW

This soup is delicious hot or cold.

WIDOW TWEED'S COZY NOG

BRIOCHE-INFUSED EGGNOG

DIFFICULTY

Prep time: 10 minutes
Resting time: 10 minutes
Cook time: 2 minutes

INGREDIENTS

Yield: 4 servings

2 large slices butter brioche
2 cups milk
4 egg yolks
½ cup sugar
½ teaspoon vanilla extract
Pinch of cinnamon

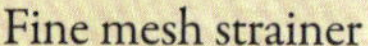

EQUIPMENT

Fine mesh strainer

Widow Tweed is a kind and compassionate person who knows and cares for every animal on her farm. This warm milk drink is just as comforting as one of her big, soft hugs.

1. First, toast the brioche in the oven or a toaster. For the best flavor, it should come out a deep golden brown.
2. Pour the milk into a saucepan and bring to a simmer. Drop in the toasted brioche, remove from the heat, and steep for 10 minutes.
3. Strain the brioche out of the milk, leaving only the flavor. Return the infused milk to the stove and warm to 175°F.
4. While the milk is heating, add the egg yolks, sugar, vanilla, and cinnamon to a mixing bowl. Whisk vigorously for 3 minutes and then pour in the hot milk, whisking continuously. Do not stop whisking until the mixture thickens into a smooth, creamy beverage.
5. Serve your eggnog piping hot!

THIS
IS
my
FAVOURITE
JAR

SUMMER IN A CUP

LEMON-LIME SODA WITH ORANGE AND GRAPE JUICE

DIFFICULTY

Prep time: 5 minutes

INGREDIENTS

Yield: 1 serving

1 tablespoon plus 1 teaspoon orange juice

¼ cup white grape juice

¼ cup plus 2 tablespoons blood orange juice

¼ cup plus 1 tablespoon lemon-lime soda

1 orange slice

A few ice cubes

There's nothing like sipping a fruity drink while you soak up the summer sun on a sandy beach. It's one of the things Olaf is most looking forward to about summer.

1. Add the orange juice and ice cubes to a tumbler glass. Pour in the white grape juice and blood orange juice. Stir with a cocktail spoon. Add the lemon-lime soda and stir again.
2. Garnish the glass with the orange slice. Enjoy right away.

TIPS

SEASONAL FRUITS AND NUTS

SPRING

Avocado
Apricots
Lemons
Bananas
Strawberries
Alpine Strawberries

Raspberries
Passion fruit
Currants
Kiwis
Litchis
Mangoes

Melons
Nectarines
Papayas
Watermelons
Peaches
Tomatoes

SUMMER

Apricots
Cranberries
Almonds
Bananas
Blackcurrants
Cherries
Chestnuts
Lemons
Quinces
Dates
Figs

Strawberries
Alpine strawberries
Raspberries
Passion fruit
Currants
Litchis
Mangoes
Melons
Mirabelle plums
Blackberries
Blueberries

Nectarines
Hazelnuts
Papayas
Watermelons
Peaches
Pears
Plums
Damson plums
Greengage plums
Tomatoes

AUTUMN

Pineapples
Avocado
Bananas
Chestnuts
Lemons
Clementines
Quinces
Dates
Figs
Passion fruit
Pomegranate
Persimmons
Kiwis
Kumquats
Litchis
Mandarins
Mangoes
Hazelnuts
Walnuts
Oranges
Grapefruits
Papayas
Pears
Apples
Plums
Damson plums
Grapes

WINTER

Pineapples
Avocado
Bananas
Lemons
Clementines
Dates
Passion fruit
Pomegranate
Persimmons
Kiwis
Litchis
Mandarins
Mangoes
Oranges
Grapefruits
Papayas
Pears
Apples

SEASONAL VEGETABLES

SPRING

Garlic
Artichokes
Asparagus
Eggplant
Beets
Swiss chard
Napa cabbage
Cauliflower
Kohlrabi
Romanesco broccoli
Cucumber
Zucchini
Watercress
Spinach
Fennel
Fava beans
Romaine lettuce
Morel mushrooms
Turnips
Peas
Dandelions
Sugar snap peas
Bell peppers
Potatoes
Radishes
Rhubarb
Frisée

SUMMER

Garlic
Artichokes
Eggplant
Leaf lettuce
Swiss chard
Broccoli
Carrots
Green cabbage
Brussels sprouts
Savoy cabbage
Kohlrabi
Romanesco broccoli
Red cabbage
Cucumber
Pickling cucumbers
Squash
Zucchini
Watercress
Fennel
Fava beans
Navy beans
Green beans
Romaine lettuce
Corn
Patty pan squash
Peas
Sugar snap peas
Bell peppers
Potatoes
Pumpkin
Radishes

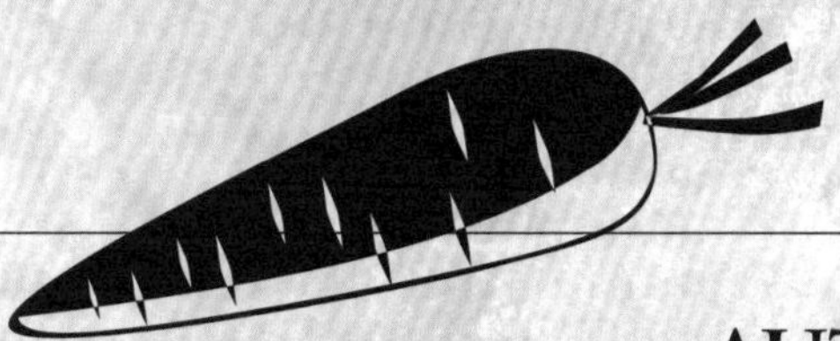

AUTUMN

Eggplant
Red beets
Swiss chard
Bolete mushrooms
Broccoli
Carrots
Celery
Celeriac
Porcini mushrooms
White button mushrooms
Green cabbage
Brussels sprouts
Savoy cabbage
Red cabbage

Cauliflower
Squash
Watercress
Shallots
Endives
Spinach
Fennel
Chanterelle mushrooms
Navy beans
Lettuce
Lentils
Mâche
Corn
Turnips

Onions
Parsnips
Oyster mushrooms
Leeks
Bell peppers
Potatoes
Red kuri squash
Pumpkin
Radishes
Rutabaga
Salsify
Jerusalem artichokes
Black trumpet mushrooms

WINTER

Beets
Carrots
Celeriac
Green cabbage
Brussels sprouts
Savoy cabbage
Red cabbage
Cauliflower
Squash

Watercress
Shallots
Endives
Spinach
Lentils
Mâche
Turnips
Onions
Parsnips

Leeks
Potatoes
Red kuri squash
Pumpkin
Salsify
Escarole
Jerusalem artichokes

STOCKS

VEGETABLE STOCK

Yield: 4 cups of stock
Prep time: 5 minutes
Cook time: 2 hours
Resting time: 30 minutes

INGREDIENTS

4 carrots
1 leek, white part only
½ stalk celery
1 onion
1 shallot
1 bouquet garni (green part of 1 leek, 4 stems parsley, 1 stalk fennel, 1 bay leaf, 1 sprig thyme)
8 cups water
⅔ cup white wine
1 star anise
3 cardamom pods

- Dice the carrots. Cut the leek, celery, onion, and shallot into small pieces.
- Place all the ingredients in a stewpot and simmer for 2 hours, covered.
- Remove stock from heat, let cool for 30 minutes and then strain.

FISH STOCK

Yield: 4 cups of stock
Prep time: 20 minutes
Cook time: 40 minutes

INGREDIENTS

2 onions
2 shallots
2 leeks
1 stalk celery
3 tablespoons unsalted butter
14 ounces fish heads and bones (ask at the fish counter)
½ cup mirin
4 cups water
1 bouquet garni (4 parsley stems, 1 fennel frond, 1 bay leaf, and 1 sprig of thyme tied in a green leek leaf)
Olive oil, for cooking

- Peel and finely chop the onions and shallots. Rinse and dice the leeks and celery.
- Pour a drizzle of olive oil into a Dutch oven along with the butter and warm over medium heat. When the butter is melted, add the fish heads and bones. Sauté for 1 minute and then add the shallots, onions, leeks, and celery. Sauté for 1 more minute before pouring in the mirin. Stir well and add water to cover. Add the bouquet garni, cover the pot, and cook over low heat for 35 minutes, skimming frequently.
- Strain out all the solids for a nice, clear fish stock.

CHICKEN STOCK

Prep time: 20 minutes
Cook time: 4 hours 15 minutes

INGREDIENTS

4½-pound chicken carcass
7 tablespoons grapeseed oil
3 tablespoons butter
1 clove garlic
2 shallots
8 cups water
1 bouquet garni (thyme and bay leaf tied in a green leek leaf)
1 sprig fresh rosemary
2 juniper berries
Pinch of crushed peppercorns

- Crush the chicken carcass and sauté it in a stewpot with the grapeseed oil and butter. Stir and cook over medium heat until the carcass turns golden brown. Remove it from the pot and set aside.
- Preheat the oven to 300°F. Skim off the fat from the cooking pot, but leave the browned bits in the pot. Cook the garlic and shallots in the stewpot for 5 minutes over medium heat, scraping up the browned bits. Remove from the heat.
- Return the chicken carcass to the stewpot, pour in the water, add the bouquet garni, and cook in the oven for 4 hours. Thirty minutes before the stock is finished cooking, add the rosemary, juniper berries, and peppercorns to the stewpot, then return it to the oven.
- These spices will add depth and flavor to your stock. After 4 hours, strain the contents of the stewpot, saving only the liquid.

SAUCES AND CONDIMENTS

MARINATED EGGS

Prep time: 5 minutes
Cook time: 6 minutes
Resting time: 5 minutes, plus at least 1 hour to marinate

INGREDIENTS

8 eggs
1⅔ cups soy sauce
1 cup water
½ cup mirin or rice vinegar
1-inch piece fresh ginger

- First, bring a pot of water to a boil. Drop in the eggs and cook for 6 minutes. While the eggs are cooking, prepare a large bowl of ice water to quickly cool them.
- Add all the other ingredients to an airtight container.
- When the eggs are done cooking, transfer them immediately to the ice water and let cool for 5 minutes, then peel them and transfer to the marinade. Close the container and refrigerate for at least 1 hour before eating.

BARBECUE SAUCE

Prep time: 10 minutes
Cook time: 30 minutes
Resting time: 15 minutes

INGREDIENTS

2 onions
1 clove garlic
1-inch piece fresh ginger
1 tablespoon grapeseed oil
2 tablespoons light brown sugar or raw cane sugar
3 tablespoons Worcestershire sauce
1 cup ketchup
Drop of liquid smoke (optional)
Pinch of salt

- First, peel and dice the onions. You can also use a food processor. Peel, de-germ, and finely chop the garlic. Peel and finely chop the ginger.
- Now you are ready to begin cooking: In a small saucepan, warm the grapeseed oil over medium heat. Drop the onion into the hot oil and sauté for 10 minutes, stirring frequently with a wooden spatula. Season with a pinch of salt and then add the sugar, garlic, and ginger. Cook for another 5 minutes, using a wooden spoon to stir. Deglaze with the Worcestershire sauce and add the ketchup.
- Stir well and then simmer over low heat for 10 minutes.
- Remove the sauce from the heat, add the liquid smoke, and stir well. Pour your barbecue sauce into an airtight jar and keep in the refrigerator.

LOBSTER BISQUE

Yield: 6 cups of bisque
Prep time: 15 minutes
Cook time: 1 hour

INGREDIENTS

2 onions
2 carrots
1 stalk celery
1 clove garlic
1 lobster, cooked and prepared
3 tablespoons unsalted butter
2 tablespoons grapeseed oil
2 tablespoons tomato paste
1 tablespoon flour
⅓ cup cognac
6 cups Fish or Vegetable Stock
2 cracked peppercorns
1 bouquet garni (4 parsley stems, 1 fennel frond, 1 bay leaf, and 1 sprig of thyme tied in a green leek leaf)
⅔ cup heavy whipping cream
Salt

- First, dice the onions, carrots, and celery. Peel, de-germ, and finely chop the garlic. When your aromatics are ready, move on to the lobster. Shell the lobster and chop the meat. Crush the lobster shell and head and set aside.

- Now you are ready to begin cooking: Add the grapeseed oil to a Dutch oven and warm over medium heat. Add the butter and melt it, then add the lobster meat, shell, and head and season with salt. Turn the heat up to medium-high and cook for 5 minutes to brown all the ingredients, using a wooden spoon or rolling pin to crush them as much as possible for the most flavor. Thoroughly stir in the tomato paste. Sprinkle with the flour.

- Deglaze with the cognac and use a wooden spoon to scrape all the browned bits off the bottom of the Dutch oven. Pour in the fish or vegetable stock and stir well. Add the cracked peppercorns and the bouquet garni.

- Cover, turn down the heat to low, and simmer for 45 minutes. After cooking, strain the contents of the pot to obtain a flavorful broth. Press the solids into the sieve or strainer to extract as much of the liquid as possible. Stir in the cream and check the seasoning. Your bisque is ready!

A LITTLE SOMETHING SWEET

HAZELNUT AND CHOCOLATE CHIP COOKIES

Yield: 16 cookies
Prep time: 15 minutes
Resting time: 1 hour 30 minutes plus 10 minutes
Cook time: 15 minutes

INGREDIENTS

1⅔ cups plus one heaping tablespoon flour
4 teaspoons baking powder
1 teaspoon cornstarch
⅔ cup hazelnut flour
Pinch of salt
¾ cup salted butter
½ cup sugar
Scant ⅔ cup brown sugar
1 whole egg plus 1 yolk
⅔ cup chocolate chips

- Combine the flour, baking powder, cornstarch, hazelnut flour, and salt in a mixing bowl.
- Melt the butter and pour it into a separate mixing bowl. Add the white and brown sugar and stir well before adding the whole egg and egg yolk. Mix again.
- Stir together the wet and dry ingredients and then mix in the chocolate chips. Your cookie dough is ready. Refrigerate for at least 1 hour 30 minutes before baking.
- While the dough is in the refrigerator, preheat the oven to 350°F. Remove the dough from the refrigerator and form it into 16 relatively large balls. Arrange them on a baking sheet lined with parchment paper. Make sure to leave plenty of space for them to expand. Bake for 15 to 20 minutes, keeping a close eye on them for doneness.
- Remove the cookies from the oven and cool for 10 minutes on a wire rack before eating or breaking into pieces as a milkshake topping.

WHIPPED CREAM

Prep time: 10 minutes

INGREDIENTS

2 cups heavy whipping cream
Scant ½ cup powdered sugar

- Making whipped cream is easy if you know the trick: Start with very cold whipping cream, and a cold mixing bowl and whisk as well. Place the mixing bowl and whisk (or electric mixer beaters) in the freezer for several minutes to make sure they are very cold.
- Add the whipping cream and powdered sugar to the mixing bowl and whisk vigorously until the whipped cream is firm and forms a peak at the end of the whisk.

VANILLA ICE CREAM

Prep time: 10 minutes
Cook time: 5 minutes
Resting time: 15 minutes
Churning time: 5 to 10 minutes

INGREDIENTS

2 cups whole milk
1 cup heavy whipping cream
2 vanilla beans
8 egg yolks
½ cup plus 1 tablespoon sugar
1 teaspoon fleur de sel
2 pounds ice cubes or crushed ice
1 cup coarse salt

- There's nothing easier than whipping up your own homemade ice cream—it only takes a few minutes and doesn't require a lot of special equipment.

- First, make a custard: Pour the milk and cream into a saucepan. Split the vanilla beans open and use the tip of a paring knife to scrape out the seeds. Add the vanilla pods and seeds to the saucepan. Bring to a boil and then remove from the heat. Leave the vanilla to steep in the milk for a few minutes before removing the pods.

- Meanwhile, add the egg yolks, sugar, and fleur de sel to a mixing bowl. Beat the egg yolks vigorously with a whisk until lighter in color. Finally, add the vanilla-infused milk one third at a time, whisking continuously.

- Pour the contents of the mixing bowl back into the saucepan and warm over medium heat. While stirring constantly (making a figure eight motion with your whisk), heat the mixture to 183°F. Monitor the temperature using a cooking thermometer, and take care not to let it exceed 183°F, or the eggs will overcook and the ice cream will be ruined. The custard is ready when it coats the back of a spoon. Pour it into a mixing bowl.

- Now, chill the custard: Pour the ice into a large mixing bowl and add the coarse salt. Mix the salt and ice, then set the mixing bowl containing the custard down into it. Whisk the custard or stir with a silicone spatula for 5 to 10 minutes. The salt will reduce the temperature of the ice from about 28°F to 3°F, which is perfect for churning your ice cream by hand.

- After you have stirred the ice cream base in the cold bowl for several minutes, you will see it thicken and transform into a delicious ice cream. Enjoy it right away, or store it in an airtight container in the freezer.

HAZELNUT PRALINE PASTE

Prep time: 25 minutes
Cook time: 15 minutes

INGREDIENTS

2 cups whole Piedmont hazelnuts
⅔ cup granulated sugar
⅔ cup powdered sugar
2½ tablespoons powdered milk (optional)
1 tablespoon grapeseed oil (optional)

- Preheat the oven to 350°F.
- First, toast the hazelnuts: Place them on a baking sheet and bake for 15 minutes. Transfer the hot hazelnuts to a clean cloth, taking care not to burn yourself. Rub them with the cloth to remove their skins. Set aside.
- Make a dry caramel: In a heavy-bottomed saucepan, melt one third of the granulated sugar over low heat. When it has melted, add another third and melt again. Finally, add the remaining granulated sugar and let it melt without stirring. Your caramel is ready when it turns a rich golden color. Line a baking sheet with parchment paper or a silicone baking mat and pour the caramel onto it. Let it cool and harden, then crush it.
- Now make the praline paste: Add the toasted hazelnuts to a blender along with the caramel pieces and blend until the mixture liquefies. Stir in the powdered sugar and powdered milk, if using. Blend until smooth.
- Blend by pulsing for 5 to 10 seconds at a time. The more you blend, the runnier it will become. Continue blending until the paste reaches your desired consistency. If it seems too dry, drizzle in grapeseed oil as needed. Transfer to an airtight container and enjoy within 7 days.
- Note: Depending on the fat content of your hazelnuts, you may not need to add oil. Giffoni or Piedmont hazelnuts, for example, have a fat content of 60% and do not require any additional oil.

APPLESAUCE

Yield: 4 servings
Prep time: 15 minutes
Cook time: 45 minutes

INGREDIENTS

6 apples
2 tablespoons salted butter
⅔ cup water
1 tablespoon lemon juice
Scant ⅔ cup light brown sugar or raw cane sugar
1 vanilla bean

- First, peel and core the apples. Cube the fruit and set aside.

- Melt the butter over medium heat in a Dutch oven. Add the apples, water, lemon juice, and sugar. Stir well and leave to simmer. Meanwhile, use a paring knife to split the vanilla bean open lengthwise. Scrape out the vanilla seeds and add them to the apple mixture, along with the pod. Stir well and cover. Simmer over low heat for 45 minutes to 1 hour.

- When the apples are fragrant and very soft, remove the vanilla pod. Smash the apples with a potato masher or blend with an immersion blender. Your applesauce is ready!

SIMPLE TWISTS ON YOUR DRINKS

COLORFUL ICE CUBES

Here are two very simple ways to make colored ice cubes.

1. FOOD COLORING

- Fill several glasses with fresh water. Add a few drops of food coloring (1 color per glass). Pour the contents of the glasses into the compartments of an ice cube tray and freeze for several hours.

2. SYRUPS

- Add 2 dashes grenadine syrup to an ice cube tray and add water. Stir with the tip of a knife or a spoon handle and then freeze for several hours.

FRUITY ICE CUBES

- You can not only add color to ice cubes, but also flavor them with fresh fruit, peel, zest, pulp, etc.

- The process is very simple. Place a piece of fresh fruit—either whole, like raspberries, or in cubes for something like pear—into each compartment of an ice cube tray and add water to fill. Freeze for several hours.

CONVERSIONS

GALLONS	QUARTS	PINTS	CUPS	FLUID OUNCES
1⁄16 gallon	¼ quart	½ pint	1 cup	8 fluid ounces
⅛ gallon	½ quart	1 pint	2 cups	16 fluid ounces
¼ gallon	1 quart	2 pints	4 cups	32 fluid ounces
½ gallon	2 quarts	4 pints	8 cups	64 fluid ounces
1 gallon	4 quarts	8 pints	16 cups	128 fluid ounces

GRAMS	OUNCES
14 grams	½ ounce
28 grams	1 ounce
57 grams	2 ounces
85 grams	3 ounces
113 grams	4 ounces
142 grams	5 ounces
170 grams	6 ounces
283 grams	10 ounces
397 grams	14 ounces
454 grams	16 ounces
907 grams	32 ounces

IMPERIAL	METRIC
1 inch	2.5 centimeters
2 inches	5 centimeters
4 inches	10 centimeters
6 inches	15 centimeters
8 inches	20 centimeters
10 inches	25 centimeters
12 inches	30 centimeters

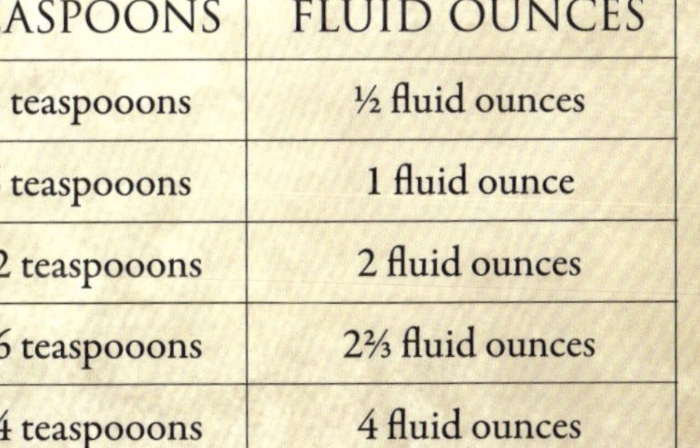

CUPS	TABLESPOONS	TEASPOONS	FLUID OUNCES
1⁄16 cup	1 tablespoon	3 teaspooons	½ fluid ounces
⅛ cup	2 tablespoons	6 teaspooons	1 fluid ounce
¼ cup	4 tablespoons	12 teaspooons	2 fluid ounces
⅓ cup	5½ tablespoons	16 teaspooons	2⅔ fluid ounces
½ cup	8 tablespoons	24 teaspooons	4 fluid ounces
⅔ cup	10⅔ tablespoons	32 teaspooons	5⅓ fluid ounces
¾ cup	12 tablespoons	36 teaspooons	6 fluid ounces
1 cup	16 tablespoons	48 teaspooons	8 fluid ounces

FAHRENHEIT	CELSIUS
200°F	93°C
225°F	107°C
250°F	121°C
275°F	135°C
300°F	149°C
325°F	163°C
350°F	177°C
375°F	191°C
400°F	204°C
425°F	218°C
450°F	232°C

GLOSSARY

B

BRUNOISE

Cut vegetables into ¼-inch cubes.

D

DEGLAZE

A technique that consists of dissolving and collecting the browned bits from the bottom of a dish or frying pan by adding a liquid, such as water, or wine at the end of cooking.

G

GELATIN

Available in sheet or powdered form, gelatin is an animal-derived gelling agent used in making candies, marshmallows, icings, etc. It can be replaced with other types of gelling agents such as agar-agar, which is plant-based.

I

IMMERSION BLENDER

This tool is very useful for preparing blended soups directly in the saucepan or in a mixing bowl. Its sharp blades can easily purée vegetables into a soup. Make sure to keep it pointed toward the bottom of the saucepan or bowl to reduce spattering.

M

MIXING BOWL

Large, round-bottomed bowl usually made of stainless steel.

R

REDUCE

Decrease the volume of a sauce, stock, or juice by cooking it at a gentle boil so that the liquid evaporates.

ROSE WATER

Product of distilling rose petals. It has a very concentrated rose fragrance and flavor and is widely used in Middle Eastern cuisine.

S

Set aside

Keep a mixture or ingredient for later use while preparing a recipe.

Simmer

Cook ingredients slowly in liquid over low heat.

T

Toast

Brown a dry ingredient, such as coffee beans, hazelnuts, or almonds, without fat to release its flavors.

Z

Zest

Use a zester or paring knife to remove the zest from a citrus fruit. The zest can be used to flavor a cream or mixture or garnish a drink.

INGREDIENT INDEX

A

ALMONDS
Mole Rivera 74–75

APPLES
Applesauce 123
Carrot Tonic. 96

APPLESAUCE
A Potion to Change Your Fate. 30

APRICOTS, DRIED
Mole Rivera 74–75

ARMAGNAC
Bonzabeast Stew 100–101

AVOCADO
Ajiaco. 78

B

BACON, SMOKED
Lucky Cat Café Ramen. 68–69

BAMBOO SHOOTS
Kumandra Soup. 46

BARBECUE SAUCE
Lucky Cat Café Ramen. 68–69

BASIL, LEAVES
Magic Potion 60
Rustic Ribollita 62

BAY LEAF
A Royal Vintage 24
Vegetable Stock 116

BISQUE, LOBSTER
Creamy Gumbo-Style Soup 38

BLUEBERRIES
A Potion to Change Your Fate. 30

BREAD, RUSTIC
Rustic Ribollita 62

BREAD, STALE
Mole Rivera 74–75
Nottingham Pottage. 80

BRIOCHE
Widow Tweed's Cozy Nog 106

BUTTERNUT SQUASH
Midnight Latte 22

C

CAPERS
Ajiaco. 78

CARCASS, CHICKEN
Chandelier Pea Soup 84
Chicken Stock 117

CARCASS, FISH
Fish Stock 116

CARDAMOM
Vegetable Stock 116

CARROTS
Bonzabeast Stew 100–101
Harvest Soup 44
Lobster Bisque. 119
Nottingham Pottage. 80
Rustic Ribollita 62
Vegetable Stock 116

CAULIFLOWER
The Soup. 82

CELERY
Creamy Gumbo-Style Soup 38
Fish Stock 116
Lobster Bisque. 119
Rustic Ribollita 62

Vegetable Stock 116

CHAMOMILE, DRIED
Soothing Nightcap 88

CHERRIES
Magic Potion 60

CHERVIL
Chandelier Pea Soup 84

CHICKEN, FARM-RAISED
Nottingham Pottage. 80

CHICKEN, TENDERLOINS
Ajiaco. 78

CHIVES
The Soup 82

CHOCOLATE CHIPS
Hazelnut and Chocolate Chip Cookies . . 120

CHOCOLATE, DARK
Mole Rivera 74–75

CHOCOLATE-HAZELNUT SPREAD
Midnight Latte 22

CILANTRO, FRESH
Ajiaco. 78
Kumandra Soup. 46

CINNAMON (STICK)
Midnight Latte 22
Mole Rivera 74–75
A Royal Vintage 24
Widow Tweed's Cozy Nog. 106

CLAMS
Bonzabeast Stew 100–101

CLEMENTINES
Herculade Citrus Twist 50

CLOVES
Mole Rivera 74–75
Nottingham Pottage. 80
A Royal Vintage 24

COCONUT CREAM
A Devious Potion 34

COCONUT WATER
Motunui Cooler 28

COD, FILLET
Zuppa Marcovaldo! 72

COFFEE
Midnight Latte 22

COGNAC
Lobster Bisque 119

COOKIES, HAZELNUT AND CHOCOLATE CHIP
Hazelnut Parsnip Whip. 32

CORN
Ajiaco. 78
Harvest Soup 44

CORNSTARCH
Hazelnut and Chocolate Chip Cookies . . 120

CREAM
Ajiaco. 78
Bonzabeast Stew 100–101
Chandelier Pea Soup 84
Harvest Soup 44

CREAM, HEAVY WHIPPING
Lobster Bisque 119
Midnight Latte 22
Vanilla Ice Cream 121
Whipped Cream 120

CROUTONS, GARLIC BREAD
Zuppa Marcovaldo! 72

CUMIN
Ajiaco 78
Creamy Gumbo-Style Soup 38

CUMIN SEEDS
Mole Rivera 74–75

D

DATES, MEDJOOL
Arabian Nights Jallab 26

E

EGGS
Hazelnut and Chocolate Chip Cookies .. 120
Marinated Eggs 118

EGGS, MARINATED
Lucky Cat Café Ramen 68–69

EGGS, YOLK
Vanilla Ice Cream 121
Widow Tweed's Cozy Nog 106

ESSENTIAL OIL, BITTER ORANGE
Soothing Nightcap 88

EXTRACT, ORANGE BLOSSOM
Black and White Boba 90

EXTRACT, PASSIONFLOWER
Soothing Nightcap 88

EXTRACT, VANILLA
Herculade Citrus Twist 50

F

FENNEL
Vegetable Stock 116
Zuppa Marcovaldo! 72

FISH, WHITE
Zuppa Marcovaldo! 72

FLOUR, HAZELNUT
Hazelnut and Chocolate Chip Cookies .. 120

FOOD COLORING
Alien Jellies 52
Wonderland Potion 98

G

GARLIC
Barbecue Sauce 118
Bonzabeast Stew 100–101
Chicken Stock 117
The Clades' Dancing Soup 104
Creamy Gumbo-Style Soup 38
Lobster Bisque 119
Mole Rivera 74–75
Nottingham Pottage 80
Rustic Ribollita 62
The Soup 82
Zuppa Marcovaldo! 72

GARNI, BOUQUET
Bonzabeast Stew 100–101
Chicken Stock 117
Fish Stock 116
Lobster Bisque 119

GELATIN POWDER
Alien Jellies 52

GINGER
Barbecue Sauce 118
Breakfast Porridge 86
Herculade Citrus Twist 50
Marinated Eggs 118
Midnight Latte 22

GRAPEFRUIT
Herculade Citrus Twist 50
Saint-Tropez Special 92

GUAVA
Motunui Cooler 28

H

HAZELNUTS
Hazelnut Praline Paste ... 122
Mole Rivera ... 74–75

HONEY
A Devious Potion ... 34
Porridge and Table Manners ... 42
Soothing Nightcap ... 88

I

ICE CREAM, VANILLA
Hazelnut Parsnip Whip ... 32

J

JAM, BLUEBERRY
A Devious Potion ... 34

JUICE, APRICOT
Saint-Tropez Special ... 92

JUICE, BLOOD ORANGE
Summer in a Cup ... 108

JUICE, CARROT
Carrot Tonic ... 96

JUICE, CRANBERRY
A Potion to Change Your Fate ... 30

JUICE, GINGER
Carrot Tonic ... 96
A Toast to Bernard! ... 54

JUICE, GRAPE
A Devious Potion ... 34
Mortality Potion ... 58
A Royal Vintage ... 24

JUICE, GRAPE (WHITE)
Summer in a Cup ... 108

JUICE, GRAPEFRUIT
Saint-Tropez Special ... 92

JUICE, ORANGE
Summer in a Cup ... 108

JUICE, PINEAPPLE
Wonderland Potion ... 98

JUICE, POMEGRANATE
A Devious Potion ... 34

JUICE, STRAWBERRY
Freeeze! ... 56

JUICE, YUZU
A Toast to Bernard! ... 54

JUJUBE, DRIED
Breakfast Porridge ... 86

JUNIPER BERRIES
Chicken Stock ... 117

K

KALE, LACINATO
Rustic Ribollita ... 62

KETCHUP
Barbecue Sauce ... 118

KIWIS
Motunui Cooler ... 28

KUMQUAT
Breakfast Porridge ... 86

L

LEEKS
Fish Stock ... 116
Vegetable Stock ... 116

LEMONGRASS (STALK)
Breakfast Porridge ... 86
Kumandra Soup ... 46

LIME
Applesauce ... 123

Herculade Citrus Twist 50
Kumandra Soup 46
Motunui Cooler 28
Surf's Up Shave Ice 65
Surf's Up Smoothie 64
A Toast to Bernard! 54
Wonderland Potion 98

LIME, LEAVES
Kumandra Soup 46

LIQUID SMOKE
Barbecue Sauce 118

LOBSTER
Bonzabeast Stew 100–101
Lobster Bisque 119

M

MANGO
Surf's Up Shave Ice 65
Surf's Up Smoothie 64

MASCARPONE
Midnight Latte 22

MILK, ALMOND
Black and White Boba 90

MILK, COCONUT
Motunui Cooler 28
Porridge and Table Manners 42

MILK, POWDERED
Hazelnut Praline Paste 122

MILK, WHOLE
Hazelnut Parsnip Whip 32
Midnight Latte 22
Vanilla Ice Cream 121
Widow Tweed's Cozy Nog 106

MINT, FRESH
Magic Potion 60
A Potion to Change Your Fate 30
The Queen's Transformation Potion 36

MIRIN
Chandelier Pea Soup 84
Fish Stock 116
Marinated Eggs 118

MISO, RED
Lucky Cat Café Ramen 68–69

MUSHROOMS, CREMINI
Breakfast Porridge 86

MUSHROOMS, SHIMEJI
Kumandra Soup 46

N

NAVY BEANS
Rustic Ribollita 62

NORI, DRIED
Lucky Cat Café Ramen 68–69

NUOC MAM
Kumandra Soup 46

O

OATS, ROLLED
Porridge and Table Manners 42

OIL, SESAME
Lucky Cat Café Ramen 68–69

ONIONS
Barbecue Sauce 118
The Clades' Dancing Soup 104
Creamy Gumbo-Style Soup 38
Fish Stock 116
Lobster Bisque 119
Mole Rivera 74–75
Nottingham Pottage 80
The Queen's Transformation Potion 36
Rustic Ribollita 62
Vegetable Stock 116

ONIONS, SPRING
Ajiaco 78
Lucky Cat Café Ramen 68–69

ORANGES
A Royal Vintage 24
Summer in a Cup 108

OREGANO, DRIED
Ajiaco 78
Mole Rivera 74–75

P

PAPRIKA
Creamy Gumbo-Style Soup 38
Harvest Soup 44

PARSLEY, FLAT-LEAF
Bonzabeast Stew 100–101
The Clades' Dancing Soup 104
Creamy Gumbo-Style Soup 38
Harvest Soup 44
Nottingham Pottage 80
The Soup 82
Vegetable Stock 116

PARSNIPS
Hazelnut Parsnip Whip 32

PEARS, BOSC
Mortality Potion 58

PEAS
Chandelier Pea Soup 84

PEPITAS
Mole Rivera 74–75

PEPPER, ANCHO
Mole Rivera 74–75

PEPPER, BELL, RED
The Clades' Dancing Soup 104
Creamy Gumbo-Style Soup 38

PEPPER, CALABRIAN
The Queen's Transformation Potion 36

PEPPER, CHILI, MILD
Ajiaco 78
Bonzabeast Stew 100–101
Creamy Gumbo-Style Soup 38

PEPPER, CHILI, MILD GREEN
The Clades' Dancing Soup 104

PEPPER, CHILI, THAI
Kumandra Soup 46

PEPPER, ESPELETTE
The Clades' Dancing Soup 104

PEPPER, MULATO
Mole Rivera 74–75

PEPPER, PASILLA
Mole Rivera 74–75

PINE NUTS
Rustic Ribollita 62

PINEAPPLE
Surf's Up Shave Ice 65
Surf's Up Smoothie 64

PISTACHIOS, UNSALTED, SHELLED
Porridge and Table Manners 42

POMEGRANATE
Mortality Potion 58

POTATOES
Ajiaco 78
Chandelier Pea Soup 84
Harvest Soup 44
Nottingham Pottage 80
The Queen's Transformation Potion 36
Rustic Ribollita 62
Zuppa Marcovaldo! 72

POTATOES, SWEET
Lucky Cat Café Ramen 68–69

PRALINE PASTE, HAZELNUT
Hazelnut Parsnip Whip 32

PURÉE, CHERRY
Wonderland Potion 98

PURÉE, PEACH
Saint-Tropez Special 92

R

RAISINS
Mole Rivera 74–75

RAMEN NOODLES
Lucky Cat Café Ramen 68–69

RASPBERRIES
Porridge and Table Manners 42

RICE, SHORT-GRAIN
Breakfast Porridge....................... 86

RICOTTA
The Queen's Transformation Potion 36

ROSE PETALS, DRIED
Porridge and Table Manners 42

ROSE WATER
Arabian Nights Jallab.................... 26
Porridge and Table Manners 42
Rustic Ribollita 62

ROSEMARY
Chicken Stock 117
The Clades' Dancing Soup 104
Rustic Ribollita 62
Zuppa Marcovaldo! 72

S

SAFFRON
Bonzabeast Stew 100–101

SAUSAGE, SMOKED
Creamy Gumbo-Style Soup 38

SESAME SEEDS
Mole Rivera 74–75

SHALLOTS
Bonzabeast Stew 100–101
Chicken Stock 117
Harvest Soup 44
Vegetable Stock 116
Zuppa Marcovaldo! 72

SHRIMP
Bonzabeast Stew 100–101
Zuppa Marcovaldo! 72

SHRIMP PASTE
Kumandra Soup.......................... 46

SODA, LEMON-LIME
Herculade Citrus Twist 50
Summer in a Cup 108
A Toast to Bernard! 54
Wonderland Potion 98

SOY SAUCE
Marinated Eggs 118
Lucky Cat Café Ramen 68–69

STAR ANISE
Herculade Citrus Twist 50
Midnight Latte 22
Mole Rivera 74–75
A Royal Vintage 24
Vegetable Stock 116

STRAWBERRIES
Freeeze! 56
Magic Potion 60
A Potion to Change Your Fate............ 30

STOCK, CHICKEN
Ajiaco................................... 78
Lucky Cat Café Ramen 68-69
Mole Rivera 74–75
The Soup 82

STOCK, FISH
Bonzabeast Stew 100–101
Creamy Gumbo-Style Soup 38
Lobster Bisque......................... 119
Zuppa Marcovaldo! 72

STOCK, VEGETABLE
Breakfast Porridge....................... 86
Chandelier Pea Soup 84
The Clades' Dancing Soup 104
Harvest Soup 44
Nottingham Pottage...................... 80
The Queen's Transformation Potion 36
Rustic Ribollita 62

SWISS CHARD (BUNCH)
Nottingham Pottage. 80

SYRUP, CHERRY
Wonderland Potion 98

SYRUP, MAPLE
Black and White Boba. 90
Lucky Cat Café Ramen 68–69
Midnight Latte 22
A Toast to Bernard! 54

SYRUP, MINT
Alien Jellies. 52

SYRUP, PEPPERMINT
A Potion to Change Your Fate. 30

T

TAPIOCA STARCH
Black and White Boba. 90

TOMATO PASTE
The Clades' Dancing Soup 104
Lobster Bisque. 119

TURMERIC
Carrot Tonic. 96

TURNIPS
Nottingham Pottage. 80

V

VERBENA, FRESH
Saint-Tropez Special. 92

W

WATERCRESS (BUNCH)
The Queen's Transformation Potion 36

WATERMELON
Freeeze! 56

WHIPPED CREAM
Hazelnut Parsnip Whip. 32

WORCESTERSHIRE SAUCE
Barbecue Sauce 118

Z

ZUCCHINI
The Clades' Dancing Soup 104

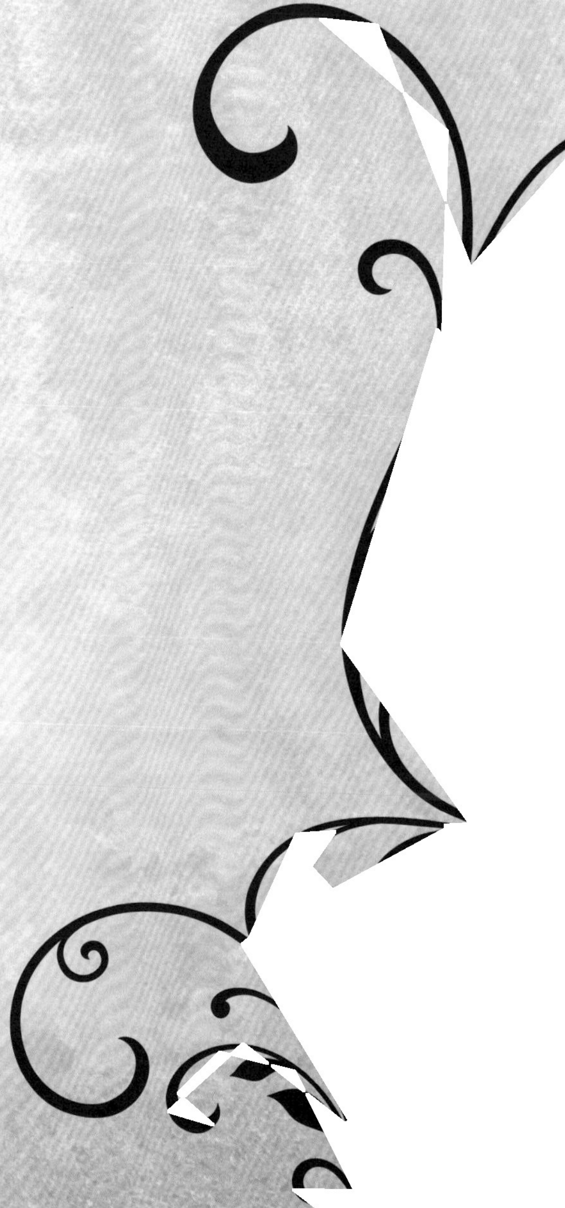

You've come to the end of *Enchanted Elixirs,* and I truly hope the book has been everything you wished for! Before you go, I would like to thank you. For 10 years now, I've been writing cookbooks inspired by incredible worlds of imagination. What a dream job! And I have you to thank, for supporting my work and coming back for more. THANK YOU!

I would also like to thank my wife, Bérengère, and my son, Henri, who share not only my love of good food but also my obsession with all things fantasy, particularly the Disney and Pixar universe. It is such a joy to share the adventure of living with both of you, and to have your support along the way.

Thank you to my sister and my parents, who have always loved and supported me. Without them, I might not have such a keen appreciation for a job well done and a hunger to experience all life has to offer.

A special nod to my aunt Paqui, who watched my very first Disney movie with me. It was *The Black Cauldron*, lesser-known film that was far too scary for a boy my age! Still, I have very fond memories of watching it with you, Aunty.

Thank you to my team—Isabelle, Baptiste, Maurane, Arthur, Paul and Paul, Pépin and Nellu, Julien and Amandine—who keep Gastronogeek on the right track. And I can't forget Fizariel, SebCafé, Korunpack, and Dantalion—thank you all!

Thank you to Nicolas and Sidonie, who once again did an amazing job reproducing iconic scenes and scenery to capture incredible photos.

Thank you to Anne, my publisher for the past 10 years, for your trust and expert guidance on these books I love to create.

Thank you to Béren for your artistic direction and everyone at Hachette Heroes for their graphic design, as well as all their hard work behind the scenes to get this book into your kitchen.

Thank you to Timothée and Catherine at Hachette Heroes for their confidence and for putting up with me this whole time. (Kudos, truly.)

Thank you to all the artists, creative minds, and Disney and Pixar employees who for so many years have been dreaming up, making, and producing the incredible movies that inspire both my recipes and my family's imagination.

Thank you.

Thibaud Villanova
Gastronogeek

PO Box 3088
San Rafael, CA 94912
www.insighteditions.com

Find us on Facebook: www.facebook.com/InsightEditions
Follow us on Instagram: @insighteditions

The Hundred and One Dalmatians is a novel by Dodie Smith published by Viking Press.

The story for *The Princess and the Frog*, copyright © 2009 Disney, is loosely based on *The Frog Princess* by E. D. Baker, copyright © 2002, published by Bloomsbury Publishing.

The characters in the Disney films *The Rescuers* and *The Rescuers Down Under* are inspired by the books by Margery Sharp, *The Rescuers* and *Miss Bianca*, published by Little, Brown and Company.

Originally published in French as *Les Elixirs Enchantés Disney* by Hachette Livre, France, in 2024. © 2024, Hachette Livre (Hachette Pratique). English translation by Lisa Molle Troyer. English translation © 2025 Insight Editions.

ISBN: 979-8-3374-0306-9

Publisher: Raoul Goff
SVP, Group Publisher: Vanessa Lopez
Editorial Director: Thom O'Hearn
Art Director: Stuart Smith
Associate Editor: Sami Alvarado
Managing Editor: Shannon Ballesteros

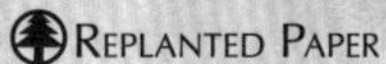

Insight Editions, in association with Roots of Peace, will plant two trees for each tree used in the manufacturing of this book.

Manufactured in China

10 9 8 7 6 5 4 3 2 1